Frank Attfield Fawkes

Marmaduke, Emperor Of Europe.

Frank Attfield Fawkes

Marmaduke, Emperor Of Europe.

ISBN/EAN: 9783744651639

Printed in Europe, USA, Canada, Australia, Japan

Cover: Foto ©ninafisch / pixelio.de

More available books at **www.hansebooks.com**

MARMADUKE,

EMPEROR OF EUROPE.

BEING

A RECORD OF SOME STRANGE ADVENTURES IN THE REMARKABLE CAREER OF A POLITICAL AND SOCIAL REFORMER WHO WAS FAMOUS AT THE COMMENCEMENT OF THE TWENTIETH CENTURY.

BY X.

CHELMSFORD:
EDMUND DURRANT & CO., 90, HIGH STREET.

LONDON:
SIMPKIN, MARSHALL, HAMILTON, KENT & CO., LD.
—
1895.

CONTENTS.

	PAGE
PROLOGUE.—Relating the peculiar manner in which the manuscript of the annexed history came into the hands of its present possessor	1
CHAPTER I.—How a book was a failure, and what the author and some of his friends had to say on the matter	9
CHAPTER II.—Arthur Hardy receives a disastrous blow and loses heart. He is much impressed by reading the account of a vision	19
CHAPTER III.—How Arthur Hardy interviewed Colonel Wolff and his friend, and how the latter appeared more impressed with the conversation than the gallant Colonel	30
CHAPTER IV.—A summer idyl, chiefly treating of birds, blossoms, and breezes; of bright sunshine; of a rural paradise; and of female loveliness	38
CHAPTER V.—An account of a grand reception, and how Arthur Hardy became a topic of discussion thereat	47
CHAPTER VI.—Showing that an accident may have unforeseen and far-reaching results	54
CHAPTER VII.—The war in Mwangesland, and the important part played in it by the new suffocating explosive "Queljanite"	63
CHAPTER VIII.—The political thunder rumbles and the war clouds gather. Will they burst over Europe in a rain of blood?	71

CONTENTS.

CHAPTER IX.—Treats chiefly of love and duty, and shows what different aspects the latter assumes when viewed from different standpoints 82

CHAPTER X.—In which the proposal of a Home Rule Bill for Alsace-Lorraine creates a great deal of astonishment 94

CHAPTER XI.—Showing how "Marmaduke" issues a manifesto, and the effect it has upon various classes of society 102

CHAPTER XII.—How some of the teachers and preachers of religion received the manifesto. A Pyrrhic victory! 111

CHAPTER XIII.—A bolt from the blue. A diabolical outrage threatens to put back the clock of progress many years 117

CHAPTER XIV.—Electioneering excitement. The battle of the ballot box and the result thereof 125

CHAPTER XV.—Relates some of the motives which actuated the policy of the German Emperor 131

CHAPTER XVI.—Showing how the course of diplomacy, like true love, does not always run smoothly 138

CHAPTER XVII.—An account of a mission undertaken by Marmaduke, and the reception which he met with 147

CHAPTER XVIII.—Marmaduke visits Paris, meets with an enthusiastic reception, and returns to Berlin exhausted, but successful 156

CHAPTER XIX.—Marmaduke recruits his health at Felixstowe, but finally hears news which greatly agitates him, and accelerates his departure 166

CHAPTER XX.—A case of mistaken identity produces disastrous results 176

CHAPTER XXI.—"The Good Samaritan" in the guise of a farm labourer 184

CHAPTER XXII.—How Marmaduke reads a categorical and circumstantial account of his own death 193

CHAPTER XXIII.—How an escritoire was broken open in the "Telephone Room" of the Imperial Palace in Berlin, and what was discovered therein 201

CHAPTER XXIV.—A little cottage at Falkenham and its inmates 211

CHAPTER XXV.—Marmaduke finds that he is compelled to be dead to the world; he therefore decides henceforth to be known as Arthur Hamilton 219

CHAPTER XXVI.—How Arthur Hamilton becomes a reporter on the staff of *The East Anglian Daily Times* 228

CHAPTER XXVII.—Gives a rapid glance at the progress of events, and tells how it is proposed to appoint a day commemorative of the life and works of Marmaduke 238

CHAPTER XXVIII.—The day of commemoration. Westminster Abbey. The crowd and the procession 246

CHAPTER XXIX.—Inside Westminster Abbey. An impressive ceremony. A startling proclamation. A mental tragedy, and an unexpected vision 252

EPILOGUE.—Five years after. On board the Orient Liner *Corangamite*. The reign of Marmaduke and the age of gold. 265

ED. DURRANT & Co.,
Printers, Chelmsford.

MARMADUKE,
EMPEROR OF EUROPE.

PROLOGUE.

RELATING THE PECULIAR MANNER IN WHICH THE MANUSCRIPT OF THE ANNEXED HISTORY CAME INTO THE HANDS OF ITS PRESENT POSSESSOR.

LET it be distinctly understood that I emphatically disclaim any responsibility for either the merits or demerits of the extraordinary narrative given in the following pages.

I regard myself as a mere conduit, through which flows to the public a stream of literary matter, which the said public, at its good-will and pleasure, may consider good, bad, indifferent, or a combination of all three.

Whether I am right or wrong in making such a disclaimer of responsibility, you, sir or madam, will be able to decide after I have related how the manuscript of this curious history came into my possession, and after you have perused the history aforesaid.

A short time ago I was returning to town by a morning train from Chelmsford, in which important provincial borough I had been spending a few days upon business connected with the assizes.

The 9.38 a.m. up express had just started, and I congratulated myself that I was sole occupant of a first-class compartment.

What selfish mortals we are! Upon calm reflection, what pleasure can there be in having six seats at our disposal when we can only occupy one, or, by turning up an arm, two?

However, congratulate myself I did, as I had some letters to read, and knew that five unoccupied seats could not, by the wildest stretch of imagination, disturb me by making inane remarks upon the weather and a hundred other trivial topics.

The train was fairly on its way, and we were passing the Widford siding, about three miles from Chelmsford, when it occurred to me that the carriage was stuffy. Both windows were closed. I opened the near side window, then crossed over and opened that on the off side, came back and resumed my seat, which was on the near side, in the corner nearest the engine, gave a glance at the five empty seats, again congratulated myself that I should have no interruption until the train reached Liverpool Street, opened my first letter and began to read it.

You will see my reason directly for mentioning such apparently insignificant details.

I suppose I had read about half the letter when I was considerably startled by a voice at my left elbow, saying:

"Excuse me, but can you tell me the day of the month?"

I looked up, and in the seat next to me, was a man dressed in black. The cut of his clothes was certainly different from anything I had ever seen, peculiar, yet not exactly old-fashioned. He had a sallow complexion, clean-shaved face, sparkling eyes, deep sunk in the sockets, high cheek bones, and a nervous restless manner. His age—well the more I come to think of it, the less am I able to say what his probable age was. At the first glance one might guess twenty-seven. Glance at him again, and the guess might be fifty. Give him another glance and one would feel morally certain that the man had lived far beyond the allotted age of three score years and ten; but that a vigorous constitution, exceptional vitality, and a regular life had successfully kept back wrinkles and other usual indications of extreme old age.

I was more than startled. A nervous shiver ran through me, and I stared at him without being able to ejaculate a word.

Again he said, "Excuse me, but can you tell me the day of the month?" Slightly recovering my presence of mind, I told him. "And the year?" I gave him the year. "I thought you would say so. Do you know, sir, that the actual date is a number of years later than the one you mention?" I mildly ventured to suggest that I knew what I was talking about. "Look out of the window," replied my strange companion. I did so, and was certainly surprised to see a large number of houses and other buildings, in fact, quite a good sized town, where a few days before, when I passed the same spot, open fields existed.

"I daresay the fashion of my dress seems peculiar to *you*, but it is the ordinary fashion of to-day; look out of the window when we pass Brentwood Station."

The whistle sounded, the speed was reduced, and we passed the station at almost walking pace. I looked out. All the men had clothes cut in the same peculiar manner as my mysterious friend, and the head-gear and costume of the women were very different from anything to which I was accustomed. After this the train resumed its usual speed.

"You see I was right."

I was obliged to confess he was, and began to think that I belonged in some mysterious manner to a bygone generation. It was dawning upon me that *I* was the mystery, not my new acquaintance.

"I don't wish to interrupt you from reading your letters, if you can find pleasure in reading stale letters many years old," said my new friend, with an evident sneer. "But I want you at your leisure to read through these records of the stirring events of the past few years. They are correct, authentic, and will give you some hitherto unpublished incidents connected with the life of a man whom most people call great. For the best of all possible reasons I know these records are correct. They may be valuable to you. When you have read them, you will probably be anxious to know who I am. Don't try to find me; your labour will be in vain. You will never see me again." With that he handed me a parcel of papers; some manuscript, some newspaper cuttings, the whole tied round with red tape. I untied the tape and glanced at the papers. The first page bore the title:

MARMADUKE,

Emperor of Europe.

Looking up, with the object of further questioning my mysterious companion, I found he had vanished!

Now, kind reader, your genial criticism, if you please. Of course I had dozed and dreamt it all. I had a heavy breakfast and somnolent dyspepsia aided my imagination. Or I imagined the interview and invented the visitor. So be it. But how about the parcel of manuscript? Fortunately, I am in possession of this valuable piece of evidence; and a sight of it will refute the "dream" theory. This manuscript at the present moment is securely locked in my fire and burglar-proof safe. Any sceptical reader is at liberty to inspect it upon giving me due notice and appointing a convenient time.

You say I overlooked the presence of the stranger when I entered the carriage. This could not be, for, as you will have remarked, I have been particularly careful to produce accurate circumstantial evidence that the compartment was empty when the train started and for some time afterwards. Besides, on this hypothesis, how can the vanishing of the stranger be accounted for?

Was I under the influence of hypnotism? I say emphatically, no! For it is now generally conceded that there is no involuntary or compulsory hypnotism, or hypnotic power over a subject, unless that subject places his or her will voluntarily at the disposal of the hypnotiser. In other words, a person cannot be hypnotised against his will. This is a fact, not an opinion. I was certainly not a willing subject, and I protest that I could not have been hypnotised against my inclination, or without my consent.

That there was something in connection with my mysterious visitant which was not capable of explanation by ordinary means, I am certain.

To tell the truth, gentle madam and kind sir, I do not intend to endeavour to account for any of the mysteries I have related. I simply state facts and there leave the matter.

The composition thus left in my hands is certainly a remarkable one. I do not know whether to regard it as a tale, a history, a dream, or an allegory.

When I first read it I must candidly confess I was disappointed. What kind of being was this "Emperor of Europe." Biassed by history I was misled. Naturally I expected that the man who made it his life work to conquer Europe, and who succeeded, would be a man of blood and iron; a man with a herculean frame; a man who would, if necessary, remorselessly sacrifice human beings; a man in whom self-interest would overwhelmingly predominate.

But I saw depicted as the central figure in this strange MS. a man who was the very reverse of this; a man with the delicate, nervous organisation of a woman; a man intensely sympathetic; a man with the gentleness of a child; a man who was burnt up with a passionate desire to benefit humanity; a man who placed humanity first and self last.

The more I pondered upon what I had read, the more I found my mind was being permeated and saturated with the subtle influence of this mysterious man. His wonderful personality was literally haunting me.

Like the Jews of old, and a great many other good people, I had formed a certain idea of what a monarch should be. This strange story told me of an Emperor of a totally different type. I was disappointed. But as I thought over and pondered upon what I had read, the truth began to dawn upon me that in "Marmaduke, Emperor of Europe," there was a monarch of a type transcendently superior to any that I had hitherto heard or read of.

However, I will not indulge in any further criticism or opinion, but will append the strange volume, exactly as it came into my possession.

As the authorship is essentially "an unknown quantity," I have announced on the title page that the work is by "X."

Let me mention one rather curious fact before I

bring this rambling prologue to an end. In examining the manuscript I found that the paper used was of various sizes, and evidently turned out by different paper mills. But upon holding some of the sheets of paper up to the light and closely scrutinising the water mark, I was startled by the discovery that in several instances a date was distinctly visible several years later than the present year of grace!

THE EDITOR.

CHAPTER I.

HOW A BOOK WAS A FAILURE, AND WHAT THE AUTHOR AND SOME OF HIS FRIENDS HAD TO SAY ON THE MATTER.

IT was a bright afternoon, on the first of August when the twentieth century was not many years old, that a young man entered the private office of the managing partner of a firm of publishers, in Paternoster Row.

This young man was about thirty years of age, slightly built, of medium height. He had a clean-shaven face (except for a slight moustache), a pale complexion, and an anxious demeanour.

His name was Arthur Hardy. His profession that of author and journalist.

Let us follow him. The conversation had already commenced, and the publisher was speaking.

"You cannot tell how sorry I am. But I can assure you, my dear sir, that we have used our utmost exertions to make your book a success. For our own sake, as well as yours, we have tried every means at our disposal to push your book to the front. We have sent a review copy to every prominent London and Provincial newspaper and magazine, and a presentation copy to a large number of leading public men. We have exhausted the limit you gave us for advertisements, and have inserted additional ones at our own expense; our travellers have specially visited the 'trade' and the big bookstall people. But for some reason or other, the book does not seem 'to catch on.' I confess I am disappointed, and regret it all the more as I feel the book on its merits ought to succeed. It gives novel, not to say startling ideas, essentially right ones, in excellent language, and in an attractive form. We have given it a good trial, but the sales, which were very limited at the outset, have now stopped, in fact, I fear we shall never get through the first edition, which, to save you expense, was purposely made a small one."

Arthur Hardy, whose usually pale face became paler still, murmured a few words of thanks to the publisher, and quitted the office.

"So," soliloquised the unhappy author, "here ends all my hopes and aspirations. Fool that I was! To dream that it was possible to raise the tone of society by a book. I might have known that society, eager with its grovelling profitmongering, its sordid schemes for getting the better of its neighbour, its selfish efforts to keep those under it down, and pull those above it under, would never respond to my feeble calls to higher life ideals. Fool that I was! How shall I tell my poor, ailing wife, my darling Avis? What will she say? All her hopes were centred in this wretched book. Her constant dream was that this book was to regenerate society, and she was continually predicting a glorious future for the book, for me, and for herself. I am afraid that the rude awaking from this dream will make her malady worse."

Leaving Arthur Hardy to think out the best way

to break the disastrous news of the failure of his book to his sick wife, we will precede him to his home.

It was a very commonplace home. The house was situated in that crowded southern suburb of the great city known as Loughboro' Junction. Hardy's home was one of several hundred of small houses, all exactly alike, and all as hideous as the combined efforts of speculator and jerry builder could make them. Each had in the front a liliputian forecourt about 3ft. 6in. deep, and, in the rear, a yard containing the minimum number of square feet allowed by the law.

The house was typical of the vast number of suburban residences which were such a standing disgrace to the last four decades of the nineteenth century. Flimsily built, they were beginning to decay, and many of them were already in a tumbledown condition.

Troubles never come alone. Our poor author had to report a failure to his sick wife, and he would have preferred to have had this interview without witnesses.

To his especial regret, however, he found his brother-in-law, Richard Bruton, awaiting him. The two brothers-in-law were not in sympathy with each other on many points, and they generally managed to ruffle each other's tempers whenever they met, and argued, as they generally did.

The wan face of the wife on the sofa, rendered still more wan by her unnaturally bright eyes, formed a striking contrast to the rubicund visage of her brother as he leaned back in a comfortable posture in an easy chair.

As Arthur Hardy proceeded with his painful recital, the only effect apparent upon the face of Richard Bruton was the gradual formation of a smile of self-satisfaction. This smile broadened until it found forcible fruition in words. "Exactly what I told you, Arthur; now didn't I prophesy all this? If you will try to build castles in the air you are bound to come down a cropper. Whoever supposed anyone would listen to your wild schemes of social reform. Bah! I'm sick of hearing of social reform. Do you suppose you're going to upset the wholesome laws of healthy competition, supply and demand, and all that sort of thing? Of course the weakest go to the wall, and who would prevent them? Let them go to the wall I say, and be rid of rubbish. 'Every man for himself, and the devil take the hindermost,' that's my motto. It's a regular divine law, and you can't help it. Fancy, ha! ha! Excuse me smiling, Arthur, but fancy trying to persuade people not to fight and go in for arbitration, et cetera. Ha! ha! The absurdity of the thing. Why I consider a jolly good battle now and then a splendid thing to clear the air, let off superfluous steam, kill some of the surplus population, and give the survivors a better chance. It's human nature to fight and you can't prevent it. Besides, war knocks a lot of buildings and houses into smithereens. Good for trade—must look after my own interests, you know. I'm a builder." Here he winked at his sister on the sofa. The bantering spirit subsided, and he became serious as he resumed: "Did you ever hear such a mad scheme as mixing up religion with trade, and social matters, and politics? Politics! of all things in the world. Just as if everyone didn't know that politics and religion are just a leetle bit too far apart to walk arm in arm comfortably. Now I have a great respect for religion; a very great respect." Here he made a pantomimic gesture which indicated that metaphorically he took off his hat to religion. "But I am content to keep religion in its proper place—parsons and Sundays and missionaries to the heathen. I'm not such a fool as to drag in religion where it's not wanted and oughtn't to go.

"People talked a good deal of rot of this kind before the nineteenth century came to an end. But here we are fairly started on another century, and what's come of such tomfoolery? Why, precious little, and a jolly good job too!

"Then again, where's your organisation? No schemes are worth tuppence nowadays that are not backed by a pretty strong organisation. Where's your social influence, where's your political influence, where's your position? Walk outside and look at this house. Well-built and lots of conveniences—I ought to know, for I built it and twenty more like it—but do you suppose you are going to get your wonderful schemes listened to, much less carried out, when you don't live in a bigger house than this, have no position and are unknown, absolutely unknown?"

The look of seriousness grew into contempt as he continued. "Besides, is it your duty to go mooning after idiotic schemes which don't pay, and never will pay, instead of trying to earn something to keep your wife in greater comfort, now she wants it worse than ever?

"My advice to you, friendly advice, mind you, is: drop dreaming like a red-hot cinder; drop everything that don't pay; let other people look after their own business. You stick to your reporting, and what you call journalistic work, which you seem to know a good deal about, although it certainly doesn't seem to bring in money that would suit my complexion.

"I've got a great respect, everybody's got a great respect, for a successful man. Look at me—a prosperous, speculative builder, with a good lot of houses, some mortgaged, but most of 'em free." And here he made another pantomimic gesture which might be taken to imply that he metaphorically took off his hat to himself.

"Look at me. Where do you think I should have been if I had gone mooning round, dreaming and trying to persuade people to act contrary to their born nature? Where should I have been if I had had a lot of scruples in business and hadn't looked pretty well after number one?"

Richard Bruton's disgust was so great that he was unable to formulate an intelligible reply to the question he had put.

Arthur never visibly winced during the ordeal to which his brother-in-law had subjected him, but this self-restraint to a man of Arthur's sensitive nature made the torture all the more excruciating.

Smarting under disappointment, it is quite possible for a courageous man to proclaim himself a coward.

Arthur quietly replied, "I am afraid you are right for once, Richard. Whether I did right or wrong in 'dreaming,' as you call it, I certainly ought to have resolutely crushed my inclinations and devoted my whole energies to providing more comforts for my darling. I see it all clearly now. You are right, Richard, and I am wrong. I must repair the mischief as best I can."

But the dialogue was soon interrupted. The bright eyes of the sick wife became more sparkling still as she broke in abruptly, "You are wrong, Arthur — you know you are wrong! Remember, dear, you are under orders from the chief. You have only to do your duty."

"Ah!" interrupted Richard, "I thought so. You belong to some wretched Socialist society with your 'chiefs' and your 'duty.'"

"No!" emphatically responded Arthur, "no. I may be a social reformer, but I am not what you call a Socialist."

It was quite true. Arthur disclaimed extreme methods. He abhorred anarchism, nihilism, and other exponents of brute force. He refused to identify himself with people who, calling themselves "socialists," advocated such mad schemes as a maximum income of five shillings a day for everyone from sovereign to pauper—general partition of property—all capital withdrawn from individuals and put under public control—abolition of all private property or ownership—and other plans which simply meant slavery for the individual.

Arthur believed in social reform, but only such reform as was just, gave to every man the equality of opportunity, and could be obtained by strictly constitutional means.

"Oh, Richard!" resumed his sister, "I am so sorry you are blind to all our hopes and sentiments. I don't blame you, I only pity you from the bottom of my heart. As to Arthur, he has given me more comforts than you are aware of; and all I require. I am only afraid he has worn himself out in earning money to give me delicacies. He has no cause whatever to reproach himself. I appreciate your brotherly anxiety on my behalf, but Arthur must entirely disregard what you say, and must never relax his efforts for one instant in the great work. I won't argue with you, Richard; it will be useless. But I am grieved that you seem oblivious to the wants of suffering humanity, blind to injustice and oppression, or you would help instead of hinder us. As for me, my comfort, or even existence, is as nothing when weighed in the scale against the faintest possibility of mitigating evil in the world.

"It is true, a great deal of fuss has been made at various times, especially towards the close of the nineteenth century, about what have been called social reforms; but these reforms only touched the fringe, the surface, and did not go to the root. Effects, rather than causes, have been attacked. That is the reason perhaps, why you, and others like you, consider that social reform has been a failure.

"Humanity still waits for the general application of the grand principle of the brotherhood of man, and all that it involves; wars still rage between employers and employed; between class and class; between nation and nation. The weak are still overborne by the strong; savage competition and increasing militarism are still eating the heart out of the nations. People are openly and increasingly saying Christianity is played out—heaven help humanity if it is—and shall you, shall I, hinder for one instant any man, however humble or however obscure, who attempts in the slightest degree to stem the torrent of evil in the world?"

A hectic flush spread over the cheeks of Avis Hardy, her eyes flashed with a sparkle not of earth, enthusiasm and excitement shook the frail form on the sofa. Husband and brother seemed spell-bound as she half raised herself on the sofa, and, in a voice tremulous with emotion, said to her husband, " For my sake, but especially for the sake of suffering humanity, never for one instant relax your efforts, Arthur dear. Never mind what discouragements you may encounter; if only one person is influenced by your efforts, that one person may be able to accomplish what you and I are powerless to effect. Scatter the seed, and if only one comes to maturity, that one may multiply a million-fold.

" I shall not, and you may not, live to see it, but I am certain that, sooner or later, the principles you are advocating will be accepted and acted upon in a more wide-spread manner than you can possibly imagine. Above all things, dear, never relax your efforts."

Exhausted with exertion and emotion, poor Avis Hardy sank back on the sofa and fainted.

At this moment the postman's double knock resounded through the house; in the excitement, however, of obtaining restoratives for his wife, Arthur allowed the letter to lie for some time on the doormat. When he subsequently saw it, opened and read it, he concluded it related to one of those numerous social functions which he was frequently asked to report. He then placed the letter in a rack with a number of other journalistic appointments.

The letter was as follows:

"9, Carlton House Terrace, London, S.W.

"August 1, 19—.

"Will Mr. Arthur Hardy please call upon Colonel Wolff at the above address, at 11 a.m., on Thursday, the 19th inst."

CHAPTER II.

ARTHUR HARDY RECEIVES A DISASTROUS BLOW AND LOSES HEART. HE IS MUCH IMPRESSED BY READING THE ACCOUNT OF A VISION.

THE exhaustion which overcame Avis Hardy did not yield to the usual remedies. Her medical attendant, who was immediately called in, feared a serious relapse. Perhaps the direct cause was the shock to the nervous system following the news of the failure of her husband's book—a project which she had so much cherished that it had become part of her very nature. Perhaps it was the excitement, consequent upon the heated discussion with her brother. Probably, however, a combination of the two, acting upon a highly sensitive nature, much weakened by the insidious inroads of chest trouble of long standing, was responsible for the breakdown Exactly how much responsibility rested with primary, and how much with secondary causes, is immaterial. Avis Hardy was in a critical condition.

Face to face with this greatest of all troubles, Arthur's recent disappointment was completely forgotten. He instinctively felt that his worst fears were about to be realised ; although the doctor, good man, gave the hopes that doctors usually give, built upon " a good constitution — great vital energy—excellent spirits—youth. Was she not only twenty-eight years old? Young people must never give up."

What gave Arthur additional distress was, that his wife's mental powers, hitherto so exceptionally bright and clear, had suddenly become clouded and dull. At first there was a disinclination to talk. Then she did not always understand what was said to her. Then a comatose state supervened with partial paralysis. Brain tissue had evidently given way, and the outlook became less hopeful. Arthur felt this keenly. He knew that whether the end came in hours or days, or could be postponed for weeks or months, the links which bound his wife with her environment were being severed one by one; and that he should never again, in this world, hold loving counsel with his kindred spirit as of yore. He knew that he was about to lose one grand incentive in life, that one mainstay of his hopes was about to be torn away.

Perhaps it was well that, in this case, there could be none of those interviews, so distressing to both, in which loving hearts are exposed to the anguish of having to tear themselves asunder.

Night succeeded day, and day night, with monotonous regularity for the lonely watcher. In passive helplessness he watched. Helping hands had been obtained, who carried out the various nursing routine and necessities cheerfully and well. Everything was done which could be done. Avis Hardy never rallied, and never recovered consciousness; but hovered between life and death; and five days after the seizure recorded in the last chapter, with her husband still watching by her side, and without making any sign to those around her, she calmly and quietly floated into the unseen. The actual transition was so peacefully made that they

> Thought her dying when she slept,
> And sleeping when she died.

* * * * * *

The loss of his wife was a harder blow to Arthur Hardy than the world ever knew. It was not merely that she was an affectionate companion — to part from an affectionate companion is sufficiently hard. It was not merely that she was a loving wife—a loving wife is sometimes soon forgotten.

Avis Hardy was her husband's inspiration. She had no children; she was, therefore, able to devote to her husband and her husband's work the whole of that energy, part of which would have been diverted elsewhere had she been a mother. Whilst he certainly had enthusiasm, zeal, energy, and power, their development and application were due in a great measure to his wife.

It was natural, therefore, that Arthur considered that his wife's death was a crushing blow, not only to his wishes and aspirations, but to his life work as a social reformer. Between Arthur Hardy and his wife existed an electric sympathy, a unity of mind, a oneness of spirit, to an exceptional degree. It startled them to find that one would give utterance to the thoughts passing in the mind of the other, not occasionally, not a mere coincidence, but frequently and generally. Both were highly sensitive; both had very keen perception; but as is very frequently the case, the wife's was the more rapid of the two. Intuition, as a rule, is more highly developed in woman than man, but with Avis Hardy intuition was more than a gift or brain development, it almost amounted to a second sight.

* * * * * *

The funeral was over. The blinds were again raised, and Arthur Hardy was compelled to turn his thoughts to everyday work and everyday duties. Amongst the most painful of the after-funeral tasks was setting the house in order, and perusing the various household accounts and other papers, many of which reminded him so acutely of the lost one. He shrank as yet from touching the desk containing her papers. However, searching one day for a tradesman's bill which he had mislaid, he opened this desk and immediately saw a long foolscap envelope directed—

"To my darling husband, to be opened by him after my death. AVIS HARDY."

It is not to be wondered that he hesitated some time before opening it. When he did he found the following were the contents:

"I do not leave a will in the ordinary acceptation of the word. What few trinkets I possess naturally belong to you, my first and only love. Should any of my few friends or my only remaining blood relative, my brother, desire a memento, by all means indulge their wish.

"Arthur, dearest, my health is rapidly failing. I know it. My time with you cannot be long. I will, therefore, commit to paper what is uppermost in my mind, in case I am, at the last, prevented from saying what I want to say by word of mouth.

"You know how anxious I am for the success of

your book; but it may fail. If so, do not be discouraged. The great cause must go on.

"You are highly organised, with lofty ideals. Like all highly organised beings, you are very sensitive. This is a condition which courts discouragement. Therefore, put forth a great mind effort. *Will* that your nerves be toughened.

"Whether the book, as a mere speculation, succeed or fail, be sure that opposition will come from all quarters and in all guises. Meet that opposition boldly.

"You will doubtless meet with ridicule. Strong temptation may urge you to depart from the path of duty. Apathy may overtake you. Plausible arguments may be used against you. You will need all your strength, all your courage, all your enthusiasm, to overcome opposition, ridicule, temptation, apathy, or argument.

"Be prepared to sacrifice inclination, pleasure, comfort, position, even life itself, if by so doing you can forward the accomplishment of your ideals. You know not what you may be called upon to sacrifice.

"My heart bleeds that when you read this I shall be what the world calls dead. I shall no longer be able to stand by your side and help you, and, through you, the good cause.

"But stop! Is this so? May I not, after giving up this body, be in a position to render you even more powerful assistance than I do now? May I not be able to merge my personality in yours, help you, guide you, warn you, protect you? I would gladly, as a separate entity, become extinct, if you and the cause would thereby benefit. To be parted by death may result in a more transcendent unity after all.

"Neither you nor I know exactly how the work may be accomplished. We need not disturb ourselves, however, on this point. Accomplished it assuredly will be.

"Possibly, very probably, the work may be taken from you and given to others. Trust the Chief, and do not repine so long as the work is done.

"I should very much like you to retain the *nom de plume* which you have adopted in your book. I mean the name of Marmaduke.

"I once had a fancy, a foolish one I admit, that the names of Marmaduke and Avis conjointly would revolutionise the world. This I now know cannot be. Still, do not give up the name which was dear to me.

"Not long ago I had a dream :

"I thought I stood upon the top of a mountain, and the world lay spread at my feet. Distance was annihilated. I could grasp in my vision a vast expanse, and yet I could see and hear the people distinctly. Endowed with Asmodean powers, I could even see into their houses and read their thoughts.

"The labourer tilling the ground was contented. He was no longer the sweated slave of some inexorable law of supply and demand. His honest toil enabled him to support his family decently. He had his due share of the comforts of life. He had no dread of the inevitable paupers' home at last, for 'Workhouses,' such as we knew them, had long ceased to exist. He knew that so long as he had worked when he was able, he had automatically provided for his own future.

"The son of the soil lived a natural, healthy, happy life.

"The only man in the whole landscape who starved, who was down-trodden, who was unhappy, was the malingerer, the skulker, the beggar.

"The farmer who went amongst his men had a light heart and a happy face. Foreign competition had no terrors for him. He was no longer crushed between the contending forces of low prices and bad seasons. He had no dread of being deprived of his just rights. He ceased to sigh for the three F's. A readjustment of the burdens of life had taken place, and he was prosperous and cheerful.

" A mist obscured my vision.

* * * * * *

" The mist disappeared and the dream was changed.

"This time a large city was at my feet. Merchants and manufacturers had no longer a careworn, harassed look. There was competition, but competition had lost its sting. There were certainly a number of rival firms, but the strong ones were helping the weak. Here, again, a readjustment of burdens seemed to have taken place. The foreigner was the friend, not the commercial enemy. The employer and employed were working along the same lines, not in opposite directions. I saw the manufacturer and the artizan. I saw rich and poor. I saw the large mansion and the humble cottage. I saw all classes, and all grades of those classes, peaceful, happy, and contented. But I looked in vain for the sweater. I looked in vain for the honest worker whose only hope was a bare existence, wearing out life in a miserable, unhealthy, indecent hovel. I looked in vain for strikes and lock-outs. I looked in vain for the millionaire piling up his millions, wrung out of the hearts' blood of half-starved wretches. These were all rendered impossible.

"Again a cloud obscured my vision.

* * * * * *

" The dream was changed.

" This time the interior of a prison was exposed to view; but it was very unlike a prison. It seemed a hive of industry. The inmates—I could hardly call them prisoners — possessed more hopefulness and cheerfulness than one usually associates with a prison. I saw no solitary confinement, no 'grinding the wind,' no punishments which debased the mind morally and physically. Everything I saw appeared to have for its object the raising of the inmates to a higher plane of life.

" Crime was being treated as a brain disease, and means were being taken, outside the prison as well as in, not only to cure this disease, but to prevent its development and extension. Hope was possible for those who were desirous of amending their lives; whilst the incorrigible, the murderer, and the anarchist were treated as hopeless lunatics, possessing a brain disease of a virulent, incurable, and highly infectious nature.

"Again a mist rolled before my eyes.

* * * * * *

" The dream was changed.

" I thought I was walking along Whitehall. A strange figure was in front of me. It was that of a man from whose shoulders hung suspended a mantle of dazzling whiteness, rendered more conspicuous by a cross worked in blood red upon it; and both white and red shone with a light not of earth. Conspicuous as was this figure, none of the passers-by took any notice of it. In the roadway, behind me, came trotting along a company of cavalry in brilliant uniforms, with furled standard, band at head and music playing. Suddenly the strange figure walked into the middle of the road and wheeled sharply round. I then saw that the same unearthly light was reflected from its countenance as from its mantle, and at the same moment I recognised that you were the mysterious stranger. You stood in the direct line of march of the cavalry. They still trotted on. The leading soldier was within a few feet of you. A horror came over me! You would be trodden under the feet of the horses! I endeavoured to cry out, to rush forward, to warn, to save you; but was powerless to move hand or foot to do so. Then a strange thing happened. You raised a small wand which you held in your hand and touched the foremost soldier. Instantly he, his accoutrements, and his horse crumbled into dust. This dust was caught by the wind, whirled into eddies and wreaths, and finally melted from sight. You touched the next soldier and the next. The result was the same. In a few minutes the troop of cavalry, the band, the instruments, the furled standards, and the horses, all had melted into airy nothingness as mist before the summer sun. Then you turned round and walked on. When you reached the Horse Guards, you stopped, glanced at the two mounted men statuesque and immobile in their niches; made as if you would touch them also with your wand, hesitated a moment, then lowered your wand and walked on.

"Then, whilst I was looking at you and wondering what would happen next, you also, in the twinkling of an eye, vanished from sight.

"Again the mist obscured my sight.

*   *   *   *   *   *

"The dream was changed.

"This time an Oriental country was before me. But, alas! peace, contentment, and happiness were absent.

"A battle was in progress. The boom of the cannon, the rattle and crash of repeating rifles and machine guns, the whir-r-r and swis-s-sh of bullets flying in clouds through the air, the mangling of the limbs, the cries of the wounded, all taking place immediately before me, formed a scene of indescribable horror.

"The combatants on one side were swarthy Orientals, who appeared to be mad with rage and despair. They were performing prodigies of valour, but were helpless before the superiority and discipline of their opponents. The combatants on the other side seemed to be composed of a strange mixture. I saw companies of various nationalities: there were Englishmen, Americans, Germans, Frenchmen, Italians, Spaniards, and soldiers of several smaller nationalities, all fighting side by side, all supporting and helping one another, obeying the same words of command. Suddenly the truth was revealed to me. These soldiers of various nationalities were the international military police punishing the persistent oppressors of a subject nation. Schemes of cruel ambition, aggression, and oppression had become impossible, and war as we know it had ceased to exist.

"My eyes were opened. I had been a witness of some of the results of the Brotherhood of Man and the Federation of Nations. The golden rule had at last obtained recognition in practical politics. Brute Force had at last abdicated its throne, and Righteousness ruled in its place.

"Clouds again rolled before me, and I awoke.

* * * * * *

"Will my dream ever be realised? and when?

"Meanwhile hope on and hope ever, dearest, and rest assured that—

> "The promised time is hastening on,
>   By prophet bards foretold,
> When with the ever circling years
>   Comes round the age of gold;
> When peace shall over all the earth
>   Its undimmed splendours fling,
> And the whole earth send back the song
>   Which now the angels sing."

CHAPTER III.

HOW ARTHUR HARDY INTERVIEWED COLONEL WOLFF AND HIS FRIEND, AND HOW THE LATTER APPEARED MORE IMPRESSED WITH THE CONVERSATION THAN THE GALLANT COLONEL.

THE morning of the 19th of August arrived, but Arthur had entirely forgotten the appointment made for this day. Usually he was extremely methodical, and for him an appointment made was a sacred duty to be performed. The letters he received requiring answers were invariably attended to by return of post. The death and funeral of his wife, however, formed a sufficiently valid reason for a departure from his usual business-like habits, but Arthur was not destined to suffer from the result of his forgetfulness. Someone came to his rescue, and that someone was the maid-of-all-work. This damsel in the pursuit of her before-breakfast work of tidying the parlour had managed, as maids-of-all-work generally do, to upset something, and this something, fortunately for Arthur, was Colonel Wolff's letter. Moreover to complete her beneficent work, the maid-of-all-work after spilling the letter on the hearthrug, left it there, and there Arthur saw it when he came down to breakfast.

There was still plenty of time to keep the appointment, and as the successor to "Big Ben" was striking eleven, Arthur Hardy knocked at the door of No. 9, Carlton House Terrace, which turned out to be the German Embassy, and inquired for Colonel Wolff.

After occupying a seat in a waiting-room for what seemed to him a very long time, he was ushered into an ante-room, and after a few moments further delay was conducted to Colonel Wolff's room. Nobody was there, and Arthur had time to look round and examine the room. It was a small room, comfortably furnished, but was essentially a business room, such as one would scarcely expect to see in the official residence of an ambassador of a great Power. There were numerous maps, and diagrams of portions of ships and machines on the walls, and models of parts of instruments of war in one corner. There were drawings and tracings on a desk, a voluminous library of copying books, and filed letters with reference numbers and dates methodically inscribed on the backs.

Presently Colonel Wolff entered. He was a pleasant-looking man, rather short and rather stout, wore spectacles, was in the undress uniform of a German officer, and might have been any age between thirty and forty. Accompanying him was an officer similarly attired. This officer was taller, handsomer, more erect than his companion; his piercing eyes and striking mien immediately riveted the attention of Arthur, who thought he had seen a somewhat similar face before, but could not remember where or when. "At any rate," thought Arthur, "whether I find him affable or not he is evidently a born aristocrat."

Colonel Wolff, who was the very essence of politeness and urbanity, and spoke remarkably good English for a German, commenced the conversation.

"Mr. Arthur Hardy, I presume?" Arthur bowed an assent.

"Well, sir, you have brought out a book, which has recently come under my notice, and my friend and I, who take an interest in social questions—you must understand, amongst our multifarious duties, we sometimes have to act as literary critics—thought we should like to have a conversation with the author of that book. My friend was away from London just then, hence my appointment for this morning. Your schemes of reform, I notice, apply to political and international as well as social questions. They are certainly striking, and in some respects novel. You will not object, I suppose, to my asking you a few questions? Thank you. My experience of authors, especially on social questions, is that they are most obliging, and I only wish the financial results of their efforts were always commensurate with the amount of trouble they take to disseminate useful information.

"In the first place, may I ask, are you working on your own lines, or is your book the outcome of the combined efforts of a number of workers for social reform? In point of fact, are you the mouthpiece of an organisation? You object to ally yourself to any organisation, and rely upon personal influence only. Exactly so. But has it not occurred to you that you stand rather at a disadvantage? The earth is a heavy mass, and my experience—purely as a journalistic critic—has led me to notice that if one wants to move the earth ever such a little in the direction of social reform, one must have considerable help, and that help concentrated and directed by means of very powerful and widespread organisation.

"Another point, while I think of it. Your book treats reforms more or less in the abstract, can you amplify this? Can you give us some concrete facts? Can you illustrate any practical methods by which the reforms you mention as necessary, may be carried out?"

A very sensitive chord had been struck in Arthur's nature.

The room, its contents, Colonel Wolff, his friend, all faded from Arthur's mental gaze. In a moment he became the enthusiast, the social reformer, the helper of the fallen, the champion of the oppressed. His pent up feelings could hardly find vent in words, as he poured forth to his two attentive listeners fragments of his cherished ideals.

He showed how society ought to be remodelled— from beneath, not from the top—radically, not superficially. He showed how the traditions of diplomacy should be disregarded, and precedents departed from, in favour of a new order of things. He showed how burdens must be readjusted, and the relations between man and man modified, before the world's wheels could run as smoothly as they ought to run. He showed how international friction and international disputes ought to be settled without recourse to war. He showed that schemes of selfish ambition, whether on the part of the rulers or of nations, were wrong, and that such schemes inevitably bore in them the seeds of their own punishment. He showed that the greatest happiness of the greatest number should be the statesman's ideal, and the people's goal.

Warming to his subject, he gave illustration after illustration of the methods which would effect the object of his hopes. Picture succeeded picture of the results which would accrue from carrying out his schemes. Visions of the future rose one after the other as he revealed his hopes. Sketched by the master hand of an artist, his airy castles appeared substantial erections.

"Such, gentlemen," concluded Arthur, "have been some of my waking dreams. You may smile at my enthusiasm" (they had both given him cause for the remark), "but I know I am right, and I am as certain as I stand here that one of these days the principles I advocate will be acknowledged and applied."

Colonel Wolff and his companion glanced at each other, both smiled, shook their heads, and the former turned to Arthur.

"I thank you, Mr. Hardy, for your remarks. The points you mention are very good and very desirable. I will venture to say that there is not a ruler in Europe who does not earnestly desire the welfare of his country. But in the very complicated conditions under which we live, how sir, how are all these good and desirable things to be carried out? That is the point. How? I am fully prepared to admit that the principles you enunciate are highly advantageous; but when you talk of their practical application, the thing is impossible, sir, impossible! The world is not yet ripe for such radical changes as you contemplate. Allow me again to thank you, Mr. Hardy, for the very pleasant conversation for which we are indebted to you. May I offer you some luncheon?"

Here the two officers made a movement which afforded a pretty clear indication to their visitor that they wished the interview to end.

Arthur rose, evidently dejected and depressed. He hesitated a moment as if scarcely knowing what to say. Suddenly his countenance changed, a flash of inspiration appeared to possess him; his head became erect, and he was once more the enthusiast. "Very well, gentlemen, we will dismiss the questions we have been discussing as mere dreams. I am afraid you are right, and that such dreams can never be realised. I have been told the same thing so many times before that I really begin to suspect that what everybody says must in this case be true. But there is one other matter which I should like to mention before I quit you, and it is this. You are both German officers, and it goes without saying you are German patriots; the future of your Empire is of great interest to you. Anything which promotes her advancement is your first care, and knowledge bearing upon such advancement which anyone, however humble, may possess, will receive your careful consideration. Is it not so?" They both bowed. "Then, dismissing questions of mere social reform for the present, suppose, gentlemen, that I have a plan to propose which will materially strengthen and consolidate the great German Empire. A plan which will effectually silence the Socialists and other disturbing elements which you well know are gaining strength and giving the Government so many anxious hours. A plan which, once for all, will place at the feet of

Germany her hereditary foe. A plan which, further, will cause France to acknowledge she is beaten by Germany. A plan which will free your country from the military incubus which is crushing her. A plan which will give your Empire a century of peace to develop her commercial and internal prosperity unchecked. A plan which will cause your Emperor to be hailed as the providence of his country, and make him a glorious landmark in history for all time. A plan which will enable him to win the blue ribbon of European politics.

"Suppose I possessed the great secret, the magic talisman which will effect all this, would you listen to me then, gentlemen?"

Colonel Wolff did not seem at all impressed with this impassioned speech, and was about to give a polite intimation that the interview was at an end. But, in the meantime, his companion had become unusually animated. He spoke for the first time during the interview, with almost as pure an accent as that of a native Englishman. "I think, Wolff, it might be as well to hear a little further what our friend has to say. I am going back almost directly, perhaps you can find quarters for him if he runs over to Berlin before long. Mr. Hardy, allow me to thank you for your kindness in keeping this appointment. I hope we shall meet again shortly. In the meantime you will consider our conversation as private. Wolff, give Mr. Hardy some lunch," and giving Arthur a cordial shake of the hand, Colonel Wolff's mysterious fellow officer passed out of the room.

As he walked away from the German Embassy

that morning, Arthur again tried to remember where he had seen this officer, whose face seemed so familiar to him, but could not succeed. "In any case," soliloquised Arthur, "I feel sure he is some distinguished individual, and one high in authority."

CHAPTER IV.

A SUMMER IDYL, CHIEFLY TREATING OF BIRDS, BLOSSOMS, AND BREEZES; OF BRIGHT SUNSHINE; OF A RURAL PARADISE; AND OF FEMALE LOVELINESS.

WE will shift the scene to the neighbourhood of Berlin. Near the small and obscure village of Altendorf, within a convenient distance from the capital, yet sufficiently far to be out of sight of the bricks and mortar, the stone and cement, the chimneys and dwellings, and the many other very desirable, but scarcely rural concomitants of a great city, there exists a compact little estate of some ten or a dozen acres in extent.

The house, built in the châlet style of architecture, may be described as cosy and comfortable rather than grand and pretentious. At the same time, there is a decided air of luxury pervading the whole domain and its appointments. Cost has evidently not been studied in making the whole property as perfect a gem of its kind as art and nature can make it.

Luxuriant creepers twine about a verandah which shades the chief reception rooms, and on each side of the main entrance stands a magnificent oleander in a rustic tub.

The grounds present a perfect specimen of landscape gardening. Opposite the verandah is a large lawn, broken here and there by specimen trees, and encircled, except at one point, by an undulating belt of foliage. A break in this foliage discloses a picturesque view of the distant landscape.

On one side a dip in the path leads to a shady leafy dell, embracing some natural rocks, over which falls the water from a picturesque little neighbouring stream.

The sweet scent of flowers lurks in the air. Silence is only broken by the warble of birds, the occasional rustle of the leaves, and the plash of the water over the rocks. The sky is cloudless, but the gentle breeze makes one forget that the sun is high in the heavens. Nature in every mood and tense is smiling and gracious. A sylvan paradise is before us.

But it must not be supposed that such an exquisite frame lacks a picture, such a golden setting lacks a gem. A girl of some two or three and twenty summers is seated, reading, under a tree on the lawn. Now it is impossible to give a verbal description, however accurate, of the girl before us, without descending to details which are essentially prosaic and commonplace; and the prosaic and the commonplace must necessarily destroy the very impression which we desire to give. The impression conveyed as one looks at this young girl under the tree is that of quiet, refined, intellectual beauty; of delicate grace and elegance in form and feature; of exquisite good taste in attire; of a rare combination of those indescribable charms which blend and harmonise in the person of a lovely and lovable girl. Such a combination is seldom seen in a daughter of one nationality, and the girl before us probably owes some of her advantages to the fact that she can claim ancestry from both Teuton and Anglo-Saxon. Let us look again. This young girl stands on the borderland of the ethereal (her diaphanous dress helps the illusion). In her the real and the ideal intertwine. But although what we are looking at is certainly a " vision " of loveliness, not for one moment is the illusion so strong as to cause us to forget the fact that we are regarding a denizen, and a very charming denizen, of earth.

Such are the impressions conveyed to the mind as one glances at the young girl seated, reading, under the tree on the lawn.

The girl is Alicia von Lebenheim, and she and her brother, Rudolf von Lebenheim (their parents have been dead some years) are hostess and host of Arthur Hardy.

Some nine or ten months have elapsed since the interview recorded in the last chapter; although not many changes have taken place. Arthur's conjecture was a correct one. Colonel Wolff's companion at the aforesaid interview proved to be no less distinguished a personage than the German Emperor. Intensely anxious to promote the welfare of the great Empire which had been bequeathed to him, he had never feared to examine personally questions affecting the units composing that Empire. In the interest of commerce and of labour he had initiated and promoted several measures, having for their object the amelioration of the condition of the workmen. But notwithstanding this, the Socialist element had given him great and increasing anxiety. He was bound to preserve the integrity of the various kingdoms which acknowledged him as their ruler. The very existence of the Empire depended upon her being able to resist and overcome any possible aggressors. Therefore a large and powerful army was an absolute necessity.

Every action taken by her formidable neighbour, whether by increasing the number of soldiers, improving the *personnel* of the army, or developing the various engines of war, necessitated a corresponding counter-action on the part of Germany.

Militarism had crowded out social questions, people were in a state of social revolt, hence the Kaiser had many anxieties, and wished to obtain all possible information regarding social movements.

To this rapid growth of militarism the Socialists gave determined opposition, and numerous classes of the community, although perhaps not in sympathy with the Socialists generally, were beginning to join them on this point only. Worried by internal as well as external troubles, and honestly anxious to meet and overcome them, the Emperor was keenly alive to any fresh movement on the part of the people. Just at this time there accidentally came under his notice an English book, by an anonymous author with the *nom de plume* " Marmaduke," discussing just those social questions and troubles which were engaging the attention of the Emperor. He commanded Colonel Wolff, then residing in London, a member of the German Diplomatic Service, to ascertain the identity of the author, and arrange for a private interview, upon a date when the Emperor expected to be in London.

Colonel Wolff procured Arthur's address from his publisher, and the interview was held at the German Embassy in London, as already explained. The Emperor wished to have some further conversations with Arthur on the subject, and the consequence was that Colonel Wolff arranged with his personal friend, Rudolf von Lebenheim, another member of the German Diplomatic Service, that he should act as Arthur's host during the Emperor's pleasure.

Arthur did not feel exactly like a stranger in a strange land. In his youth loving parents, not blessed with much of this world's goods, had sacrificed a great deal in order that he might have as good an education as possible; and amongst his numerous accomplishments was a very fair knowledge of French and German. Practice made him still more proficient.

At first he was in high spirits. He thought his schemes were going to be carried out forthwith. He had several interviews with His Imperial Majesty, to whom he gave long explanations, and for whom he prepared elaborate reports. The Kaiser listened attentively and graciously, but nothing further came of these interviews or reports. Arthur worked hard. With the assistance of numerous clerks from Government offices, he collated and analysed elaborate statistics connected with social and other questions, but nothing further came of the elaborate statistics.

Meantime, life at the Altendorf Villa was very pleasant.

Of society (with a large S), Arthur saw but little. Von Lebenheim's diplomatic duties were not such as obliged him necessarily to take part in High Society functions. And his sister did not care for society in the ordinary acceptation of the term. Yet both brother and sister by no means lived lives of seclusion. They were not without numerous friends whom they visited and received. Altogether Arthur lived a very happy life, far happier than if he had been compelled to take part in the stiff and formal functions of Court life.

Sometimes during the long winter evenings which succeeded his advent at Altendorf, when no visitors happened to be staying in the house, the trio would sit round the fire and indulge in conversation, heavy or light as the fancy possessed them. Arthur enjoyed these quiet evenings, for he would now and again be asked to talk upon his favourite topics, social and political reform, and explain some of his pet projects. Von Lebenheim would good-humouredly banter and chaff Arthur upon his "wild schemes"; and Alicia would frequently join in the argument and take the side of her guest against her brother. She took care, however, to make it pretty clear that she did so because Arthur was her guest, and not because she approved either of his principles or his plans. Still Arthur found it very pleasant to have the fair Alicia on his side, even with this qualification.

Sometimes Colonel Wolff would transform the trio into a quartette. Strange to say, notwithstanding the gallant colonel's agreeable manners—and they were invariably very agreeable—for some unknown reason there always seemed to exist points of antipathy between him and Arthur.

Attached to the villa was a large open-roof room. It was called a "music room," but was devoted to many more purposes besides music. At one end it contained a very good, two manual, 20-stop organ, besides other musical instruments. One also noticed here and there microscopes and other philosophical instruments; at the end, in front of the organ, was a stage which could be used for musical performances or amateur theatricals. Or a screen could be rolled down and friends could witness dissolving views and other optical experiments.

Von Lebenheim's hobby and recreation ran in the direction of music, science, optical illusions, lantern and other realistic effects. He would illustrate the latest discoveries in science, or reproduce the latest triumphs of pictorial art. His friends and acquaintances knew that when they visited Herr von Lebenheim they were certain to be entertained and amused.

Such a life was particularly fascinating to Arthur, who was an enthusiastic amateur scientist, and was also a proficient musician.

As a performer on the organ, what he lacked in excellence of execution was more than compensated for by the manner in which he imparted to the simplest melody that indescribable quality of expression which we try to express by the word "soul."

No one could hear Arthur play without being instantly aware that one was listening to a musical genius of a high order.

Therefore, it is not surprising that both Von Lebenheim and his sister were delighted with Arthur. In fact, Alicia often declared that she could listen for hours to Arthur's improvisations upon the organ, and it gave Arthur double pleasure to gratify his love for music and entertain his fair hostess.

As time wore on Arthur found, much to his surprise, that a certain development was taking place within him. He was still consumed with zeal, still keen, still sensitive, but he had become more collected, more self-possessed, firmer, and his whole moral fibre seemed to have become toughened to a degree which he had thought impossible. He felt as if he had the protection of some invisible coat-of-mail, and that he could endure whatever befell with an equanimity hitherto denied to him. His brain seemed suddenly to have become more fertile, more capable of grasping great questions and of solving intricate problems. He seemed all at once to have emerged from a chrysalis state, and become some nobler, better, stronger being.

He often wondered, with a thrill, whether the wish of his lost love, Avis, had been gratified and her personality had been merged into his, and that he was now endowed with duplicate strength and double personality.

So the time passed. Winter succeeded autumn, and spring winter; and with the beautiful summer weather Arthur still found himself under the ægis of the German Emperor, and a guest at the pleasant villa at Altendorf.

Just now we saw Alicia sitting, reading, under a tree on the lawn. Presently Arthur emerged from the house and approached her. She laid down her book, smiled, rose and accompanied him along the serpentine walks and round the clumps of foliage, through the dell and by the side of the pretty little stream. They were evidently on good terms with each other. For he found the society of his hostess decidedly agreeable. Moreover, he was dimly conscious that he was a favourite with the fair Alicia. This he inferred by those innumerable polite attentions by which ladies can so delicately indicate their preference, without in the slightest degree compromising their dignity, or over-stepping, by the smallest hair's-breadth, the line of etiquette or the limit of prudence.

He worked hard. But the life at the villa, the garden, the general environment, not to mention the companionship of Alicia, formed a refreshing relief to the monotony and worry of blue books, analysing statistics, working out details and drafting reports.

Time sped on. Pleasant walks and pleasant conversations were frequent. Arthur's ideals seemed as far from realisation as ever. Yet he was much more contented than he had ever imagined he could have been under such disappointment and discouragement.

It was quite true that Arthur was rather a favourite of Alicia. Not that he made any specific or conscious attempt to ingratiate himself with his hostess. But kindness begets kindness, and he could no more help being kind, helpful, sympathetic to everyone with whom he came in contact than he could help breathing.

He was just as keen as ever for his pet reforms, but he began to think that, after all, life has pleasures and recreations which go far to compensate one, even if cherished ideals are never realised, fond hopes are destined to be frustrated, and desired reforms are never carried out.

CHAPTER V.

AN ACCOUNT OF A GRAND RECEPTION—AND HOW ARTHUR HARDY BECAME A TOPIC OF DISCUSSION THEREAT.

THERE was a grand reception at the palace of Prince Reussenberg in Berlin. Rank, talent, and beauty were well represented. Many of the leading men of the Empire were there. Leading men, not so much as regards rank, as intellect and influence. Prince Reussenberg was by no means inclined to despise members of the nobility. On the contrary, these were always to be seen at his receptions. But he was essentially a patron of fine arts, of learning, of high development of brain power, no matter where it was to be found. At one of the Prince's receptions, therefore, the guests invariably expected to meet some of the most distinguished men of the art world; some of the literary lions; a few of the shining lights of journalism; those leading statesmen who were able to attend; some of the notable military leaders; and some professional men, including a few of the giants of astronomy, chemistry, and geography, as well as their wives, daughters, or sisters. These reunions were always brilliant, always popular, and of great utility in affording means of pleasant interchange of views amongst leading minds.

At these receptions informal discussions upon

various topics also frequently took place, especially upon any questions which happened to be then uppermost in the public mind.

The importance of Prince Reussenberg's receptions was universally acknowledged.

The particular reception to which we have alluded was no exception to the rule. It was as brilliant as usual. It was remarked, however, that no royal personages were present; all those invited had for some reason been prevented from gracing the reception with their presence.

A mere enumeration of the names of the guests would occupy more space than we have at our disposal, and further, would answer no useful purpose. But if we carefully scan the numerous throngs of visitors, we shall, after some little difficulty, be able to recognise our old friends Colonel Wolff, Rudolph von Lebenheim, and his charming sister, although however closely we scrutinise, we shall fail to see Arthur Hardy.

Conversation between the groups of visitors was animated. The units composing those groups were in constant motion. The ever-changing, intermingling colours of brilliant uniforms and sparkling toilettes produced an effect which was quite dazzling and kaleidoscopic.

The reception was at its zenith. Most of those who were expected had arrived, and very few had departed, when the word was quietly passed to about twenty of his guests that the prince requested their presence for a few minutes in the red drawing-room, a room devoted to the informal discussions already mentioned, and not usually thrown open to the general visitors. Arrived at the red drawing-room, the prince apologised for asking any of his friends to withdraw from the general assembly even for a few minutes, but intimated that he had had a conversation with his friend, Colonel Wolff, upon one or two matters, and it had just occurred to both of them that it might be desirable if these matters were communicated to those present.

Colonel Wolff rose and said that as he happened to be the only one who knew the story from beginning to end, he had been urged by his noble host to tell it.

He then gave a short account of Arthur Hardy's appearance on the scene, and of his subsequent instalment, at the Emperor's expense, as Herr von Lebenheim's guest at Altendorf, and continued:

"I should not have considered this gentleman's wild schemes and socialistic dreams worthy of the slightest regard—they would, like all other similar dreams, die a natural death—if it were not for a curious circumstance, and it is this:

"Mysterious hints have been recently thrown out and vague rumours circulated, all pointing to some great socialistic revolution. These rumours have appeared at various places, and under various circumstances, not openly or in the Press, but in an undefined intangible manner.

"For once the police are at fault and are unable to track these rumours to their source. Some are to the effect that a vast and powerful secret society, permeating the whole of the empire, is rapidly developing a line of policy which will come as a surprise to the community. In other rumours the proletariat is told to hope and watch. Another report gives out that a single brain is responsible for the direction and control of some enormous conspiracy. A further rumour says that the organisation existing for the same purpose is hydra-headed, with centres all over the empire; each centre working perfectly independently and separately, but all aiming at one result.

"But the curious and significant part is that all these rumours, though differing in details, show unanimity on one point, namely, that the organisation, or the person, or the society, or the conspiracy, or whatever it is, has for its watchword or pseudonym 'Marmaduke,' the identical name adopted by Arthur Hardy in his book. Of one thing I am absolutely certain, that he is not the author of these rumours, nor is he even aware of them. I am also equally certain that he is not associated with any society or organisation, as he considers it part of his religious duty simply to endeavour to exert personal influence, and places himself outside any organisation whatever.

"Now it may be merely a curious coincidence, and the one 'Marmaduke' may not have any connection with the other 'Marmaduke,' or the Socialists may be using our friend's *nom de plume* for their own purposes.

"Looking, however, to the fact of Herr Hardy's personal interviews with the Emperor; looking to the fact of the coincidence which I have mentioned, I thought it right to bring the matter before you.

"I need not point out the critical condition in which Germany finds herself at the present moment.

"A neighbouring nation is developing her military strength to the utmost, and openly boasting that she has at length reached and surpassed the military resources of the German Empire. There can be but one object and one aim in such boasts. You know that war clouds are now threatening to burst; added to this, Socialism within our borders has attained an audacity hitherto considered impossible. A parley, therefore, with Socialism or Socialistic ideas at the present juncture might be fatal to the best interests, nay, the very integrity of the Empire. Our duty, therefore, is to be prepared to protect our beloved Emperor and our Fatherland from what may prove to be the most insidious, and, therefore, his and our worst enemies.

"You have had the whole story. You will be the best judges if what I have related possess any importance or not."

When Colonel Wolff sat down, a grey-haired officer, the well-known and universally respected General Börsig rose, and said—

"I am sure we are all indebted to you, sir, for your interesting narrative. At the same time I do not think there is any cause for undue anxiety. It is certainly no secret that neither the Emperor nor His Majesty's advisers would give the slightest countenance to Socialistic ideas, especially at the present time; and I—I always have, and always will, hold Socialism the bitterest enemy to the Empire." Here the veteran General touched the hilt of his sword. "My decided opinion is, do not advertise this Herr Hardy. Let him severely alone, and let the Socialists stew in their own juice." (Murmurs of general approval.) "We must not forget that a bill is now before the Reichstag—a bill which the patriotism of the nation will, nay must, pass into law, by which, as you know, power will be given to make the German Army the greatest military force on the Continent. I am violating no confidence when I state that this bill once passed, every adult capable of bearing arms will be immediately called out, and such is the state of our preparedness for war that let the enemies of Germany look out for themselves. Our colleagues who are responsible for foreign affairs and for ensuring by their excellent diplomacy that contingent enemies shall be transformed into allies or neutrals, have not been idle, I can assure you, I, for one, have no fear for the future."

Scarcely had General Börsig ceased speaking, when Professor Raupp, head Analyst and Director of the Government Chemical Laboratories, rose.

"Pardon me for interpolating a word, but I should like to make a statement of an interesting, and, I believe, of a reassuring character. I have been, for some long time past, conducting experiments regarding explosives, and I am very pleased to say that these experiments have resulted in such success that for practical purposes Germany is now in possession of a propelling material which is smokeless in action, has remarkable penetrating power, only weighs one quarter of that now in use, is not affected by moisture, and is much nearer perfection than the explosive materials employed by any other nation. Of course the secret of this new explosive will be rigidly guarded by the German Government. I can congratulate the country upon the possession of a propelling explosive far superior to any other."

This statement created a certain amount of

sensation, for although it was known experiments in various explosives were being carried out, the results had been kept a profound secret. Herr Professor Doctor Raupp stood so high in his profession, was so reticent, so reliable, and possessed such a widespread reputation for never uttering a word which he could not thoroughly substantiate, that a statement by him at once received the stamp of authority, and was acknowledged as an established fact.

One or two brief speeches by leading editors and others followed.

All, without exception, expressed the most determined opposition to the Socialists in general and to Arthur Hardy in particular, his ideas, his schemes, and to whatever influence he might have exerted or would exert over any person or persons within the confines of the mighty German Empire.

CHAPTER VI.

SHOWING THAT AN ACCIDENT MAY HAVE UNFORESEEN AND FAR-REACHING RESULTS.

A FEW days after Prince Reussenberg's reception, the following appeared in a late edition of some of the London evening papers:

EXPLOSION IN BERLIN.

"About eleven o'clock this morning an explosion occurred in the experimental wing of the Government Laboratories here. Some of the upper windows and frames were blown out and several of the assistants were forcibly ejected through some of the windows. Fortunately, they fell on some shrubs, and it is believed that they have not sustained any serious injury."

Before nightfall, however, there was some amount of excitement at the London clubs in consequence of some private telegrams received; although it was difficult to ascertain what was the actual cause of the excitement. The next morning the following detailed account appeared in the *Daily News*:

"THE EXPLOSION IN BERLIN.

"MYSTERIOUS RESULTS.

"GREAT LOSS OF LIFE ANTICIPATED.

"[FROM OUR CORRESPONDENT.]

"BERLIN, Monday Night.

"Great excitement prevails in Berlin to-night. It is feared that the explosion, which at first was not considered of a serious character, has resulted in fearful loss of life. When the explosion first occurred, the only external damage visible was the ejectment of several windows and their frames. Dr. Knaus, Professor Raupp's chief assistant, was one of those who were thrown from the windows, but falling into some trees escaped with slight injuries. Neither smoke nor flame was visible; but bystanders remarked that after the explosion no one was seen to issue from the building affected. This was a remarkable occurrence, as it was known that some forty or fifty persons were in the building at the time, and uninjured inmates are usually eager to leave a building when an explosion takes place. Several persons who were in the vicinity rushed into the building from motives of curiosity, or to render help, but did not reappear. The alarm was soon received at the nearest fire-station, and the firemen were quickly on the spot; several entered the building, whilst some placed fire-escapes against the walls and attempted to enter by the window openings from which the sashes had been blown. But the moment they reached the levels of these openings they dropped to the ground as if paralysed. Although neither smoke nor flame was to be seen, some deadly invisible gases were evidently pouring from the window openings; for of seven firemen who ascended the ladders, three were evidently dead before they reached the ground, and the remaining four were so affected by the suffocating fumes that they were instantly rendered unconscious, and are not expected to recover. Besides this, the injuries they received in falling were terrible. In the meantime the firemen and others who entered the building did not re-appear; and fears are entertained that the whole of the unfortunate people who were in the building at the time of the explosion, as well as those who entered afterwards, have been suffocated. Thousands of persons have assembled in the vicinity, and the excitement is intense, as it was known that Professor Raupp and a number of other scientific men, all leading lights in the world of German science, as well as a large staff of skilled assistants were in the laboratories conducting some of the final experiments with the new improved army service explosives of which we have heard so much lately.

"The fire-engines have been for some time throwing large quantities of water on to the building and through the windows, with the object of dispersing the noxious gases.

"I have just had an interview with Dr. Knaus, the assistant who was blown through one of the windows, and miraculously escaped with very slight injuries. It is believed that he is one of the very few survivors of what, it is feared, will prove to be one of the most terrible disasters of modern times. He lies at the nearest hospital. He appeared dazed, but was sufficiently collected to explain to me that he could not account either for the original generation of the deadly gas or its constant production. It is a mystery to him. Professor Raupp, several scientific experts, and a number of assistants were analysing portions of some of the new explosive, but he was not aware of anything in either this substance or anything else contained in the building which would cause the generation of any such poisonous gases as were evidently pouring from the building. In fact, he knew of no gas which, under the same conditions, would produce the instantaneous and fatal effect observed with the unfortunate firemen.

"LATER.

"Since telegraphing, the mystery has increased. Notwithstanding the enormous quantity of water which has been thrown upon and into the building, the deadly gases are increasing in volume, and at the moment of telegraphing there is an absolute zone of poisonous gas round the building, extending fourteen or fifteen feet from the walls. Several persons who have ventured within this zone have instantaneously dropped dead. The generation of the gases must be proceeding to an enormous extent. Excitement is increasing. The experts are at a loss what to do in the face of an enemy which is so deadly, so powerful, works in such a secret, mysterious manner, and is, moreover, invisible."

The next day the following *Daily News* telegram was eagerly scanned:

"THE TERRIBLE DISASTER IN BERLIN.

"Heroic Attempt to Solve the Mystery.

" Further Details.

"[From our Correspondent.]

" Berlin, Tuesday night.

"The worst fears are confirmed. No one has yet been able to approach the ill-fated building, and it is needless to say that no hopes are now entertained that any of the unfortunate persons in the building are alive. I annex a list, supplied by the authorities, of all those who were believed to be in the building at the time of the explosion. Dr. Knaus, although still suffering from the effects of the explosion and the fall, has heroically volunteered to attempt to solve the mystery in the only manner possible, namely, by donning a diver's helmet and suit, which in this case must be made air, instead of water, tight, and having the air supplied to him by the ordinary diving-pump and apparatus, modified to suit the altered contions of pressure. Thus equipped, he considers he will be able to pass into the building without being affected by the poisonous gases. To prepare this experiment naturally occupies some time, and I am afraid the result will not be known in time for me to telegraph to night.

"LATER.

"Dr. Knaus has carried out his experiment with such rapidity and success that he has been able to visit all parts of the building. He says the sight which met his eyes at every step was sickening. Dead bodies lay around in every direction, and in almost every room. They had evidently dropped immediately they came in contact with the deadly gas, and it is satisfactory to know that death must have been practically painless as well as instantaneous, for in no case do the features exhibit traces of distortion. All have a calm, placid, and, in some cases, a pleasing expression. The explosion itself must have been very insignificant, as there are scarcely any traces of damage to furniture or building. There had evidently been neither flame nor smoke. Dr. Knaus's most successful discovery, however, was that of several portions of the explosive upon which the savants had been experimenting, *still in a violent state of ebullition*, and evidently throwing off a large volume of gas, the nature of which the explorer—although a man of the highest attainments in analytical chemistry—still professes utter ignorance.

"The constant and rapid generation of this gas will account for the mysterious manner in which it hung round the building, formed a poisonous zone, neutralised all efforts to disperse it, and, for the time being, appeared to set at naught the well-known law of the diffusion of gases.

"Now that the mystery is solved, thanks to

the courage and skill of Dr. Knaus, immediate steps will be taken for the removal of the victims."

A great many further details and telegrams appeared in the London papers during the next few days. Then the matter, like all nine days' wonders, gradually dropped into oblivion.

Two or three months afterwards *The Times* published a communication from its Berlin correspondent. This was evidently inspired, and created a profound impression. It was to the following effect:

"I understand that the appalling accident which happened a few months ago at the Government laboratories here, although disastrous in its direct consequences, will, in all probability, result in considerable advantages to the Empire.

"It will be remembered that of all those experts who held the secrets connected with the new explosives, the sole survivor was Professor Raupp's chief assistant, Dr. Knaus, and that this gentleman, at considerable personal risk, was the first to enter the building and solve the mystery of the calamity. Dr. Knaus shortly afterwards resumed his experiments and ascertained the precise nature of, and conditions under which the substance gave off large volumes of a hitherto unknown and deadly poisonous gas. Continuing these experiments, he has now been able to elaborate means by which shells can be filled with a certain chemical substance and projected from an ordinary piece of ordnance. When the shells burst the contents will be scattered in all directions, and wherever it falls it will commence *and continue for some considerable time to generate* the invisible, deadly poisonous gas, of which we had such sad experience at the laboratories.

"No visible indication whatever is given of its presence, but, as we already know, the moment a portion, however small, enters the lungs of a person, and before he is aware of its existence, he instantly drops dead.

"Escape from its effect is therefore impossible. A few such shells well placed will mean instant death to any men or horses within a considerable area.

"An army possessed of such a terrible means of destruction, which gives no warning and from which there is no escape, will be rendered, for all practical purposes, invulnerable and invincible.

"There have been several inventions in shells, having for their object the dispersion of poisonous gases upon explosion. Paul Reihm produced a shell which generated volumes of smoke wherever it exploded, and made those in its vicinity sneeze and cough. Another inventor produced a gun which was worked by electricity and was supposed to discharge per minute 5,000 projectiles, each of which was filled with a chemical preparation, which, upon the projectile exploding, discharged a poisonous, suffocating gas. There have also been the so-called cyanogen or suffocating bombs. But all these inventions broke down at a certain point, in consequence of the beneficent law of the diffusion of gases. In each case probably a suffocating gas was produced; but from the moment it was generated it commenced automatically to mix with the atmospheric air and rapidly became innocuous.

"In all the above-mentioned cases there was an exceedingly slight chance that a person would inhale the gas in a sufficiently concentrated and poisonous condition to produce injury which would result in death.

"But with the new explosive it is quite different. Dilutation with atmospheric air does not seem to materially lessen its poisonous properties; added to which, the gas is not merely generated upon the explosion of the projectile, but, as I have already mentioned, it continues to be generated in large volumes for some time afterwards.

"I understand the new explosive is to be called Queljanite.* For obvious reasons I cannot give you more detailed information.

"Of course, the most elaborate precautions have been taken to preserve inviolable the secret of this new invention. Its importance to the German Army and the German Empire, especially at the present juncture of European politics, cannot be over-estimated.

"It is understood that high honours are in store for Dr. Knaus, for his brilliant series of discoveries and inventions."

---

* "Queljanite," from Old High German "Queljan," to kill.

CHAPTER VII.

THE WAR IN MWANGESALAND, AND THE IMPORTANT PART PLAYED IN IT BY THE NEW SUFFOCATING EXPLOSIVE "QUELJANITE."

SHORTLY after the authoritative announcement regarding the new suffocating explosive, *Queljanite*, had appeared in *The Times*, the Imperial German Government were engaged in one of those little wars which one or other of the European nations almost always has in hand.

It is needless to dilate upon the exact origin of this particular little war. The starting points of all wars between great nations and semi-barbarous tribes have a curiously similar history. The overweening ambition, the truculent impertinence, the audacious effrontery of the semi-barbarous tribe must, in the best interests of civilisation, be checked by the great nation. And so war ensues.

Mwangesi, the king of the Mwangesa, a warlike tribe in Eastern Africa, and sovereign of a territory within the sphere of Germany's influence, had seen fit to put at defiance political morality in general, and German diplomacy in particular. A German expedition was therefore despatched against Mwangesi. Now this dusky monarch was a cute sovereign. He had managed to get hold of a Spaniard who had a smattering of military drill. So Mwangesi's warriors were duly introduced to western military discipline.

Mwangesi was more cute still. He had managed to arm a large proportion of his impi with Winchester repeating rifles (many of them were American manufacturers' wasters).

The king of Mwangesaland had for some time been the terror of all the neighbouring tribes, and fearful tales abounded in the surrounding districts regarding the prowess of his victorious impi. Altogether he was considered a most formidable power by his neighbours.

Cute as he was, however, unfortunately Mwangesi was not cute enough. He was puffed up with pride, and considered his impi invincible. Still more unfortunately, this military pride caused him to be so foolish as to defy the Imperial German Government. Hence the expedition. But the Government was rather more anxious than governments of first-class powers usually are in expeditions of this character.

In the first place, although a barbarian, the King of Mwangesaland was not a foe to be despised, and swamps and jungle made part of his territory almost inaccessible.

In the second place this was deemed a fitting opportunity to test the new "Queljanite," the success or failure of which, in action, naturally imparted to the expedition an importance which it would otherwise not have attained.

Accordingly extra care was taken in organisation. Officers and men were picked. The arms were proved thoroughly efficient. Every detail was carefully thought out, and the well-known and experienced

General Herz was in command. Ample precautions were taken to ensure success independently of the new explosive.

The General and a few of his most reliable officers were the only persons in the expedition who knew that a number of cases, not to be opened until the arrival of the force at its destination, contained a quantity of Queljanite shells adapted for the quick-firing machine-guns, a battery of which was invariably sent with such expeditions.

To preserve the secrecy of the operations, and to ensure that the Government should have control of all information, no newspaper correspondents were allowed to accompany the expedition; and soon after its departure a general order was issued forbidding officers or men from acting as press correspondents, or divulging military operations in their private letters.

The press was therefore entirely dependent upon official sources for all news.

A number of telegrams appeared in the newspapers recording the progress of the expedition, its arrival at the coast, its journey up country, and its arrival at Mwangesaland.

The next telegram cursorily announced, in the *Reichsanzeiger*, the meeting with Mwangesi's warriors and the result of the final engagement in the following terms:

> "Have encountered impi. General engagement held. Mwangesi thoroughly crushed, vast number killed. Survivors cowed. Conclusive victory. Our side, none killed; two officers, thirteen men wounded. Further details follow.
> "HERZ, General Commanding,"

Following upon this, the headquarter staff in Berlin received another report, marked "Special and private," of which a few excerpts are annexed.

"REPORT *RE* MARCH INTO MWAN-GESALAND AND FINAL ENGAGEMENT.

"Reliable guides, consisting of friendly natives, who were sworn foes to Mwangesi, having been obtained, a most tedious march took place. The path taken by the German force skirted some very dangerous swamps, requiring extreme caution in conducting the men, as well as the mules carrying the machine guns and the ammunition. Alternating with morasses were dense forests, thickly wooded and entangled with creepers, through which progress was extremely slow.

* * * * * *

"Only a very few natives were encountered, and these were unarmed. They were examined by our native guides, who elicited the information that a great impi of the Mwangesa was collecting at a spot of open ground on the edge of the forest, well-known to our guides. This was found to be correct, as after three days' arduous labour we reached the confines of the forest, where we found a wide stream, fordable with difficulty, between us and a clear tract of country, where we were informed the impi was collected.

* * * * * *

"Mwangesi had evidently obtained a good strategic position, for in his rear was good cover in case he found it necessary to retreat ; clear country between him and us ; and behind us the wide stream already mentioned. The impi was estimated to number about 10,000 men.

"Our force took up a position about 2,000 yards in front of this impi, which spread out in usual African custom in the shape of a crescent.

* * * * * *

"We advanced slowly, and opened fire with our machine guns, Of the seven quick-firing machine guns, it was decided that two should be used with ordinary ammunition and kept in reserve in case of necessity. The remaining five were served with Queljanite shells. The fuses of some of these were timed to explode at 2,000 yards, some at 2,500 yards, and some at 1,500, and the shells were loaded with Queljanite, having a strength of 45 (*i.e.* would continue generating the gas for a period of 45 minutes.)

* * * * * *

"When we had arrived within 2,000 yards of the front of the Mwangesa impi we opened fire with the Queljanite, only making a small advance at the end of every five or six minutes. The effect of distributing our fire in the shape of a fan, of advancing slowly, and of adjusting the time fuses for different distances, was that, within a very few minutes the Queljanite had been distributed over a very large area in the shape of an irregular circle. An area, in fact, which embraced the greater portion of the vast impi.

* * * * * *

"The effect was almost magical. There

was no smoke, very little noise, nothing to be seen; the shells were small, and their outer envelope thin. They were constructed to suffocate, not wound, consequently, as they exploded, the shell was blown into fragments too minute to be seen.

"All that was visible was an innumerable number of small flashes, each accompained by a sharp crack, immediately over the heads of the devoted impi.

"At first the dusky warriors in front made the signal for a rush. But they had not run many yards before the Queljanite began to do its deadly work. They simply dropped and died as they dropped. Not a muscle moved, not a nerve quivered when once a man fell. He was as if struck by the hand of heaven.

"Very soon the influence of the Queljanite gas extended. It was beginning to make itself felt over the whole area. There were very few spaces in the area in which the poisonous gas was not supreme. The sight was appalling. Hundreds of Mwangesa were falling in all directions. No smoke, scarcely any noise, scarcely any sound, no wounding, no writhing, gasping men. Simply men falling down dead by hundreds without any visible agency.

* * * * * *

"When the firing first commenced, the extreme ends of the horns of the crescent were entirely outside the zone of fire; and it was from these points that the firing came which caused the wounds to our officers and men, mentioned in my first telegram. But when the men forming the horns of the crescent saw their comrades in the centre simply dropping in masses, the horror of the situation overcame them, and they, as well as those who had escaped the influence of the Queljanite in the central portion of the army, threw down their weapons and shrieked for mercy.

*   *   *   *   *   *

"We counted over 5,000 Mwangesa dead on the field. Of wounded there were none. Of fugitives but a very few. The King and all his chief men were killed.

"It is needless to say the Mwangesa as opponents of Germany exist no longer.

"HERZ, General Commanding."

The Queljanite had succeeded beyond the most sanguine expectations of the Government.

There was no longer any reason for preventing this success from being published. At the same time it was not thought desirable that minute details regarding the action and effects of this new deadly weapon should reach the other European Governments. For in the deadly competition which existed in all military matters, no country could afford to expose its hand to its opponents. A report was therefore published in the *Reichsanzeiger*, stating in general terms that from information received from the commander of the expedition, Queljanite had been used with signal success during the engagement, that a large number of deaths had resulted from it, and that the short and decisive character of the engagement was due to its use.

This news was joyfully received by the general public, who felt, what the Emperor and Government knew still better, that Queljanite would give them a distinct advantage over any other nation, if not over any combination of nations, in the next war in which Germany was engaged.

Arthur Hardy was accorded the privilege of reading the foregoing private and special report, and as he perused it his heart sank within him, for he instinctively felt that German militarism had received a new and important accession of strength. He recognised in Queljanite the most formidable opponent his projects for peace had ever encountered.

CHAPTER VIII.

THE POLITICAL THUNDER RUMBLES AND THE WAR CLOUDS GATHER. WILL THEY BURST OVER EUROPE IN A RAIN OF BLOOD?

THE little household at Altendorf was in a state of great excitement. Rudolf von Lebenheim had just arrived and announced to his sister and Arthur that the Government had obtained a large majority in the Reichstag for the great Army Bill.

Von Lebenheim was in a jubilant state. His evident satisfaction found a vent in good-humoured raillery at Arthur and all his ideas. In fact Von Lebenheim was absolutely bubbling over with good-natured, very good-natured, chaff.

After he had had some refreshment, of which he stood in need, he took possession of the easiest of the easy chairs, leaned back in it as much as its construction would allow, and gave his two auditors a racy account of the enthusiastic passing of the great Bill.

He joked Arthur upon the evident utter annihilation of all his pet schemes for ensuring universal peace, was sarcastic upon the impotency of anyone who would, at the present juncture, attempt to throw a wet blanket upon the patriotism of the German nation; and offered to bet Arthur anything, from a pfennig to the jewels in the Imperial Crown, that within two months he would throw up the sponge and go in for inventing military appliances by the score for the benefit of the German Empire in general and his friend the Emperor in particular, in the forthcoming great war. Ceasing the raillery and sarcasm and wit, Von Lebenheim then dropped into a more serious vein and gave his attentive listeners a remarkably clear idea of the present political situation which had led up to the passing of the famous Army Bill. So explicit was his recital and so very undiplomatic the frankness with which he spoke of the motives which underlay the actions of statesmen and nations—a frankness so different from his habitual diplomatic reserve—that Alicia was startled and felt that there was some strong reason for such frankness. For her brother was a diplomatist and an exceedingly astute one.

It is not necessary to recapitulate the whole of Von Lebenheim's recital, but a *résumé* is all that is required for the purpose of this present history.

Commencing with France, he pointed out that at the commencement of the last decade of the nineteenth century, it was considered that the French nation had settled down to a general acceptance of her position as decided by the war of 1870-1, and had no desire to force on a war for the purpose of regaining the lost provinces. Since then, France had used every exertion to increase the efficiency of her military resources.

It is true, that, notwithstanding the enormous sums spent upon them, the much vaunted and much dreaded flying machines, which were to revolutionise warfare, were a total failure for military purposes.

But every available invention in smokeless and

improved explosives, magazine rifles, multiple machine-guns, and other instruments and material for destroying life in the most expeditious and effective manner, had been eagerly absorbed by the French Government. Gradually, but continuously, the army grew in numbers; and great strides were made in discipline and education for both officers and men. The intelligence department was carried to a high state of perfection. Organisation all round was enormously improved. Mobilisation was rendered as easy and as rapid as possible. In a word, the fighting machine was brought to a high state of development and perfection. The time had now come when all other interests were subordinated to the military interest to such an enormous extent, that France could not sustain the tension much longer. The French Government, believing that it had reached high water mark in military matters, knowing that the explosion could not long be delayed, and wishing to force on a conflict without incurring the odium and responsibility of doing so, had allowed some of its supporters to brag and bluster, and the people seemed to have caught the infection. The French nation seemed suddenly to have awoke to the belief, and indeed the hope, that war was imminent.

"In the meantime," said Von Lebenheim, "what has been the position and progress of Germany? Making a shrewd guess at what France would do, we brought in an Army Bill in 1893. This did a great deal for us at the time. We soothed the susceptibilities of Alsace-Lorraine at that time, and have continued to do so since with great success. For we have succeeded in transforming what was a solid anti-

German vote in the Alsatian constituencies in 1894 into a 75 per cent. majority for the Government to-day. We have had instant and accurate information of every step which France has taken. We possess full details of every invention adopted by our neighbours. Their mysterious secrets are no secrets so far as we are concerned. Using this information we have even handicapped some of their inventions by improving them for our own purposes. By spending enormous sums of money and concentrating an enormous amount of energy and technical skill on our navy and its adjuncts, we have succeeded in bringing ourselves more on a level with France on the sea than we ever were before. Still I candidly confess that although we have generally succeeded in keeping ahead of our friends the enemy, yet they have been too near our heels to please either the Emperor or his advisers. One thing remained to us to do, and that was to make a grand spurt. We made this spurt by bringing forward (with great trepidation, I can assure you) our great Army Bill. Our arguments were plausible, and the nation rose to the bait, you know with what success. This bill gives the executive even greater powers than the nation fully appreciates. We can now call up every man (I had almost said every woman and child) and spend every mark in military excursions and alarums. No one knows, except those in the secret, the enormous military stores which have been accumulating. The tension will shortly become so great that war will be inevitable. Having made this spurt we are anxious to take advantage of it before the other side can make a corresponding spurt.

"On the top of this comes the grand discovery of the new suffocating explosive. A discovery which, while we hold the monopoly, renders our arms invulnerable and invincible. Can we be in a more favourable condition for the coming war? So much for the military problem.

"But there is another quite as pressing and almost as important, and that is the financial problem. The enormous sums which have been absorbed by the armies and navies of Europe have made the question for more than one country—bankruptcy or war.

"There is still another problem, and that is the social one. Look this problem fairly and squarely in the face, and you must acknowledge how helpless and hopeless your milk-and-water schemes are to solve such a problem.

"In 1895 and the few following years the pendulum certainly swung both in Germany and France in the direction of social reforms. The worker and the handicraftsman received a certain amount of worship from all parties, but since then militarism has gradually succeeded in diverting the attention of both Governments from social questions to itself. Of late years the prosperity of the worker has been gradually diminishing; he has had to support in an increasing degree the military non-worker. Taxation has increased by leaps and bounds, social grievances have been pigeon-holed, and the workers' cry of distress has been either disregarded or suppressed; consequently the tension between capital and labour has become greater than it ever was before. The struggle for supremacy between capital and labour has developed to an extent undreamt of in the last decade of the last century, keen as the struggle was then.

"The position of the worker has been gradually sinking, until life for him now means not a series of efforts for reform, for comforts, for something better and nobler; with the great mass of the people, life has become a hand-to-hand fight with death for mere existence. Instead of describing how the poor live, we have now simply to relate how the poor die. I candidly tell you, that if war does not ensue very shortly, we shall have a social revolution. Germany and France are in perfect agreement on one point, viz., that to stifle the voice of the aggrieved proletariat, imminent war is an absolute necessity.

"As regards the diplomatic problem, well, we have made sure of every other country which has not made an offensive and defensive alliance with us. Russia, if she does not mind, will land herself into a mess. The hopes raised at the commencement of the Czar's reign, hopes that the grip of an iron hand would be relaxed, that Russia would be granted some measure of representative government, that moderate reforms would be introduced, have not been realised. Bureaucracy and the Orthodox Church have been too strong for the Czar, strong as this monarch is. An extensive and continuous sowing of the flourishing weeds of Siberia, the knout, judicial and administrative corruption, religious persecution, official kidnapping, imprisonment and punishment without trial, and general repression, suppression, and oppression, has resulted in such a beautiful crop of Nihilists, and other discontented gentry, that, much to her own astonishment, she will discover that her power as a factor in European politics, when put to the test, will be extremely limited. A policy of promoting the greatest misery of the greatest number can have but one result. Only one thing can save Russia from a catastrophe, and that is an up-to-date constitution, representative government, and judicious reforms.

"Besides this, we have managed to scare England to such an extent that she firmly believes Russia has felonious intentions on her Indian Empire. We have only to pull the trigger, and a judicious little plot will be hatched on the Afghan frontier—quite of Russian origin, you understand—and England and Russia will be at each other's throats. We shall put in a word of sympathy for England, and of execration for Russia, produce a secret treaty with England bearing upon this particular contingency, and presto! our powerful neighbour England is practically our ally.

"Again, take the Mediterranean and the Baltic. A secret treaty exists between England and Italy, to meet the contingency of a Franco-Russian naval alliance. We have not made an offensive and defensive alliance with England. We have done better. We have made it absolutely certain that England shall engage in war whenever it suits our convenience, and that her foes shall be our foes ; and this in spite of the fact that she has paraded her full determination to remain neutral.

"So that you see we have provided for all contingencies. Your International Peace Association has made superhuman efforts to induce the various Continental nations to take under consideration arbitration and disarmament, and copy the examples of England and America. What has been the diplomatic response to these appeals?

"France says, 'I am defending myself against the possible aggression of Germany.'

"Germany says, 'I fear, and must provide against, a war of revenge on the part of France.'

"Russia says, * 'The triple alliance is hostile to France and Russia. Let Germany and France come to an understanding, and let Austria express herself ready to leave the whole Balkan Peninsula to its legitimate owners, the Slavs and Turks; we will then consider disarmament.'

"Other countries say they are powerless to take action until France, Germany, and Russia take the initiative.

"No better proof of the strained relations between nations can be adduced than the eager manner in which every point of etiquette between rulers or statesmen of different nations is discussed in the newspapers. Congratulations are showered all round whenever polite, strictly polite, attentions are bestowed by one monarch or statesman on another, which does not wound the susceptibilities of a third.

"So you see, my dear Arthur," continued Von Lebenheim, "that a slightly more powerful agent than your interesting personality is required to stop the course of inevitable events. The sooner you recognise that you have about as much power to make for peace, as a square inch of tissue-paper has to arrest the speed of a heavy locomotive running

* *Vide* the terms of the Franco-Russian agreement prepared by MM. Flourens, Goblet, and Ribot, and concluded by M. Develle.

sixty miles an hour, the better. I grant that the question has assumed lately such formidable and fearful aspects that there is not a ruler or statesman in Europe who would not gladly be relieved of the incubus of war, *if he only knew how.*

"Depend upon it, Arthur, that the military system is as fixed in the world's economy as the laws of light, heat, or gravitation.*

"There are numerous fingers pointing to war, and immediate war: the extraordinary preparedness of Germany for war; the certainty of civil revolt; commercial paralysis; foreign complications; impossibility of maintaining the military tension; international bankruptcy."

Von Lebenheim spoke truly. These various conditions dovetailed so much one within each other, they acted and re-acted upon each other so much, that they could all be spoken of equally as causes or effects. An enormous deal of attention had been given to social questions. The Government was earnestly desirous (as indeed were other governments) of making the life of the workers as comfortable as possible. But militarism had neutralised this desire. Militarism had made such rapid growth of late years that at last it threatened to cripple commerce, paralyse industry, eat up the accumulated savings of millions, extract the comforts of life from millions more, and render existence unbearable for further millions.

* " Militarism at this hour of the day is something which can no more be eluded than the laws of gravitation. . . . We are convinced that the passing of the German Army Bill should be rejoiced over by all sincere lovers of the peace of the world."—*The Standard* on the German Army Bill, 1893.

Discontent was not unknown even in the army. The system of conscription, carried to its utmost limits, was fruitful in oppression of privates by officers; redress was difficult, revenge was awful, suicide was on the increase.*

As regards Alsace-Lorraine, it was quite true that the anti-German feeling had subsided. But Von Lebenheim did not tell Arthur what was equally true, namely, that discontent was not extinguished, but was smouldering under the surface, hidden from view, and that at the slightest touch the fire of French feeling would burst into flame over the whole of the conquered provinces.

In the midst of all these horrors of discontent, social revolution, and impending war, the Anarchists were well to the fore. Not content with the old-fashioned rule of revenge of an " eye for an eye, and a tooth for a tooth," they openly advocated twenty eyes for one, twenty heads for one.† They preached with increasing force the gospel of bloodshed and brute force; the very gospel which in rulers and armies they denounced with such energy. Truly war seemed inevitable. People were accustomed to talk in the early nineties of the strain of the military system on the resources of Europe, but the strain then was nothing compared to the strain since the close of the nineteenth century.

Militarism had indeed reached its apotheosis.

* *The Times* in 1893 admitted that since 1870 the Imperial Diet had continually passed resolutions in favour of reform in the Prussian military tribunals, but "as yet nothing has been done."

† In South Place Chapel, Finsbury, November 10th, 1893, Samuel and Nichols both advocated twenty eyes for an eye, twenty heads for one.

Militarism, however, was its own Nemesis. The anticipation of war and the preparation for it, had brought Germany, as well as other European countries, to the verge of ruin. European Governments were between the devil and the deep sea. Social revolution or war? Commercial ruin or war? Such were the dread alternatives. And war once declared, as Arthur well knew, meant a European Armageddon.

How would it all end?

*   *   *   *   *   *

Alicia was in high spirits. Whether this was caused by the triumphant passing of the great Army Bill, whether she was slightly infected with her brother's military enthusiasm, or whether it was relief and pleasure at the thought that Arthur's pet schemes—to her objectionable—were certainly destined to be relegated to obscurity, we cannot say; she was certainly in high spirits, and did not seek to hide them. On the other hand, Arthur naturally felt depressed at a secret, irrepressible conviction that his many labours were destined to be in vain, and that his cherished ideals seemed further from realisation than ever. This depression, again, was mitigated by the pleasant environment in which he found himself, an environment in which, if the truth must be told, the fair Alicia's presence occupied a not inconsiderable portion.

CHAPTER IX.

TREATS CHIEFLY OF LOVE AND DUTY, AND SHOWS WHAT DIFFERENT ASPECTS THE LATTER ASSUMES WHEN VIEWED FROM DIFFERENT STANDPOINTS.

PROBABLY both reader and author are by this time a little tired of the contemplation of Europe as one vast camp, of the smell of strange and fearful explosives, of the sight of perfected engines of war, and of the noise of millions of armed men preparing for a deadly fray. We therefore propose to give our sensory nerves a temporary relief from such sanguinary exciting causes, while we pay a visit of a private nature to the little household at Altendorf, and see what its inmates are doing.

As we pass through the entrance gates we seem to leave the din and bustle of the world far behind.

Once within its boundaries all is peace, contentment, and comfort, not to mention a certain amount of what a great many people in the world would call luxury.

Von Lebenheim is away on his diplomatic duties. Arthur, for the moment, has no work in hand. He is now in the garden, and we can see him pacing the winding paths, as he listens to the warble of birds, and unconsciously absorbs the fragrance which floats in the air. He passes the grotto, skirts the dell, and drinks in nature's loveliness with every breath. He stops still for a moment.

He feels rather sad, for he has just received news of the sudden death by apoplexy of his brother-in-law, Richard Bruton.

There had been no sympathy and very little companionship between the brothers-in-law. Richard had not always treated his sister's husband with much consideration. But true to his instinct, Arthur had always exhibited a kindly spirit, and sought by innumerable little delicate attentions to win the affection of his wife's only brother, but his advances were generally received with indifference, and sometimes repulsed with brutal coarseness.

Notwithstanding this, however, when the news of Richard's death arrived, Arthur seemed more than ever alone in the world. There remained to him now no near relative, either of himself or his wife. It is true he possessed some distant relatives, but he had heard nothing either of or from them for several years. For in years gone by, during Arthur's childhood, there had been a family feud between them and his parents. When Arthur grew up he ascertained the address of these distant relatives, and endeavoured to effect a reconciliation; but his letters remained unanswered.

Arthur resumes his walk. Presently he approaches the house, and as he passes by the side of the verandah, he glances through the French casements of the morning-room, stops for a moment, and contemplates Alicia, who is busily engaged writing.

We will leave Arthur to continue his perambulations, whilst we enter the room and glance over the shoulder of the fair Alicia.

She has just finished writing a letter to her particular and bosom friend, and proceeds to read it through in order to dot the i's and cross the t's wherever this tedious but necessary operation is necessary.

It runs as follows:

"MY DEAR ADELA,—I have delayed replying to your letter, written some long time ago, in which you ask me to give you my opinion regarding our strange visitor, Herr Hardy, until I could answer it truthfully and accurately.

"Strange to say, the longer I have delayed my answer, the more difficult seems to be my task. My judgment finds very little in his favour. He is a foreigner. In his own country he has evidently not moved in social circles equal to ours. But the chief cause of my unfavourable opinion of the gentleman, is based upon the exceedingly peculiar ideas which he holds, and the very strange schemes which he is desirous of carrying out. And, to make matters worse, he is terribly in earnest.

"How the Emperor ever came to allow his already too-worried and over-active brain to be further worried with such wild ideas as Arthur Hardy manages to concoct, is a mystery to me. Rudolf and I hold these ideas and schemes visionary, impracticable, and crude; but, independently of their imperfect character, they are all more or less Socialistic. You know I always had a horror of making too much of the lower classes. I consider the proletariat should be kept down with a firm hand. In my opinion there is little to choose between Socialism and Anarchism. Both are formidable enemies to the State. Arthur says he is not a Socialist but a social reformer. I cannot draw such fine distinctions, and cannot accept such a statement.

"The more I hear of Herr Arthur's chimerical schemes the more am I surprised with myself that I do not hate the author of them. And yet, curious to say, the longer Arthur stays with us the greater pleasure I seem to take in conversing with him. In fact, I often catch myself joining in his defence when Rudolf or Colonel Wolff are opposing him in argument. There must be some strange fascination in his ideas, for my judgment condemns what my intellect encourages. It will certainly be a great relief to me when he is gone (from what Rudolf hears, I do not think it will be long before this time arrives); at the same time I know I shall miss this strange enthusiast.

"You know I have moved in the highest circles. I have come in contact with men of higher birth, more brilliant, more intellectual, more learned, more polite, and better conversationalists; but not one who has given me so much food for reflection and thought.

"I have omitted to mention one trait in his character, which may account for my liking him in spite of my better judgment. This trait consists in the extraordinary amount of sympathy he evinces for all with whom he comes in contact. He seems to have an automatic and involuntary nervous system where sympathy is concerned, or help is wanted. The moment he sees that someone wants assistance, whether Rudolf or I, Gretchen the cook, or Hans the gardener, Arthur seems to think that he is specially appointed to render such assistance then and there. The desire to help, no matter where and no matter when, lands him sometimes in ridiculous situations, but I really think that in such circumstances the more ridiculous he appears the better I like him.

"So much for my opinion of Herr Arthur Hardy. But I verily believe, my dear, you will be unable to gather from this letter whether I like the man or not, whether I approve of his ideas or no, or whether I shall be glad to see him depart or the reverse.

"Such vacillation is quite foreign to the Alicia with whom you were acquainted. She was always accustomed to decide promptly, give good reasons for her decisions, and adhere to them.

"However, you must make the best you can of this rigmarole of a letter. When I am in a position to give you a clearer analysis of my opinion of Arthur I will write again. In the meantime I shall ever be,

"Your loving friend,
"ALICIA VON LEBENHEIM."

Having finished her letter, Alicia joined Arthur in the garden. He was standing near the dell listening to the "plash, plash" of the little cascade, and when he saw her approach him he advanced to meet her.

Did it ever strike you, reader, that a man may be in personal intimacy with a fascinating woman for a long time; that love may gradually develop until it attain the dimensions of an absorbing passion; and yet that the man may be in absolute ignorance that he is "in love"? Yet this was exactly what had occurred to Arthur. Without his being aware of it, Alicia had occupied a gradually increasing share in his thoughts, his attentions, and finally in his affections. But it was not until this morning, when he advanced to meet her near the dell, that the thought suddenly flashed across him—"I love her," and the plash, plash of the cascade seemed to re-echo the words, "I love her." In a moment his whole bearing towards her was altered. Not that he had the slightest intention of showing this alteration, but in his eyes the Alicia of ten minutes ago when he glanced through the casement, and the Alicia, of now, were different individuals. The sun was there before, but it had now risen and bathed his whole soul in a flood of light.

They sauntered slowly along the paths near the dell. A thrill passed through Arthur as he touched the arm of the new Alicia, and the "plash, plash," of the cascade seemed to Arthur's ears to say with such vivid distinctness "I love her," that his face flushed at hearing his thoughts audibly repeated.

They were both inclined to be silent, for Arthur had such a rush of thoughts leaping and tumbling tumultuously through his brain, that he had but little inclination for conversation. And Alicia felt that there was something agitating Arthur which she could not comprehend. Yet notwithstanding this ignorance, her heart beat faster. Why, she could not tell. Such conversation as they carried on was upon the most commonplace of topics.

Alicia could speak English just about as well as Arthur could speak German, and her pretty accent, when addressing him in his mother tongue, made her more enchanting than ever.

Side by side, they paced the winding paths, and for a short time nothing had been said by either of them. The dell had been left behind them and the "plash, plash," of the cascade had grown fainter and fainter until it ceased to be audible. Presently in their circuit, they again approached the dell. The "plash, plash," again made itself heard, and by the time they reached the dell, the "I love her," "I love her," of the cascade was beating into Arthur's ear and brain with an irresistible force.

He could bear it no longer. Stopping close to the cascade, swinging round in front of her and taking both her hands in his, he said calmly and forcibly—

"Alicia, I love you!"

He did not pour out any voluble protestations of affection. He did not ask her if she returned his love. His thoughts and feelings were too powerful for words. He simply looked her full in the face, waited a few moments and then repeated, "Alicia, I love you."

She released her hands from his, took his arm and half guided by her they continued their walk along the garden paths. She took a few steps in silence, and then said—

"Arthur, a few minutes ago I tried to analyse my

feelings regarding you, without success. I could not determine whether I even liked you or not. But, Arthur, I did not perhaps know it then, but," and her voice trembled, " I now know the feeling I had towards you must have been that of love."

He would have taken her to his arms, but she gently repulsed him.

"No, Arthur, I must not speak of love, unless—unless——" and here she faltered.

"I am torn between conflicting emotions. I would fain say, 'Arthur dear, I love you,' but I cannot —I cannot : there are other considerations."

"What are they, Alicia? Are they questions of position, of income, of social standing. Only say you love me, and I promise you I will not say another word on the subject till I can claim you before all the world as an equal."

"The considerations I mean are none of these. I may tell you at once, Arthur, that social distinction would never weigh with me ; money I have enough and to spare. I could never love a man if I did not thoroughly respect him, and respect stands on a higher plane than any so-called social inequalities. Dismiss all these points from your mind. No ; there is only one obstacle between us ; but duty, and duty only, compels me to ask you to remove that obstacle before I can say my heart and hand are yours. I could never unite myself to a Socialist." She shuddered at the thought. "Give up your Socialist schemes ; promise to abandon those chimerical ideas, which after all can never be realised, and the only obstacle to our happiness will disappear."

"But, Alicia, have you not frequently taken my

side in an argumentative discussion with your brother?"

"Yes, it is true; but I am afraid my heart sometimes took me where my head could not follow. My eyes are now open. I loved you and scarcely knew it. I was impelled against my judgment to argue in your favour and in your behalf. But I now know I could not be happy with you if you still adhered to your Socialist plans. Believe me, Arthur, if you wish to be happy yourself and to render me happy, do as I suggest. After all, you would be giving up very little. Has the Emperor ever given you the slightest hope that he will ever look favourably upon your mad schemes? You know as well as I do that war is inevitable—no one can now prevent it. Once let war be declared, and several generations must pass before such schemes as yours can again obtain a hearing. I have given you the alternative, and cannot withdraw it, even if my heart break."

Her eyes became moist, so did those of Arthur.

"Look at this letter," she resumed, "which my brother received this morning. It is a proposal of marriage from Colonel Wolff. I have already asked Rudolf to reply in the negative."

If the face of Alicia was lovely when in repose and under ordinary circumstances, how much more enchanting was that same face when under the spell of emotions so powerful as those which had moved her during the last few minutes. If Arthur was in love with her when she advanced to meet him at the dell, he was ten times more in love with her now. He had never seen till now what her features were capable of expressing. He was aware that she spoke the truth when she told him that the realisation of his plans was almost beyond the range of human possibility. The development of events had gradually but firmly impressed upon him the all but insurmountable nature of the obstacles to the task which he had undertaken — the all but unattainable dynamic force which would be required to make headway against those obstacles.

He felt that, after all, he was asked to give up but little. Fate, in opposing his scheme and thwarting his plans, had taken from him the substance. All he was required to do now was to yield the shadow. On the one hand, an adherence to his former principles meant political and social failure, and the loss of Alicia. On the other hand, his verbal severance from that which had already been taken away from him meant Alicia and happiness. By yielding he could lose nothing and gain everything. Love had taken complete possession of him, intoxicated him. Temptation was irresistible. He was about to give a token of his submission to fate and Alicia by clasping the fair girl to his breast when he thought he heard a voice, apparently close to him, softly and distinctly utter the word "Arthur!"

Alicia started. "What was that? Did you hear anything? I thought I heard someone say 'Arthur.' But no one is near. Was it a bird or the wind among the trees?"

Arthur was more than startled, he became deadly pale, and for a moment steadied himself against a jutting piece of rock, for he recognised the voice. It was a voice that had been dumb for many months, a voice which Arthur had never thought to hear again, the voice of his dead wife!

But whether the voice came from within or without, whether it was an actual audible utterance emanating from the spirit of his dead Avis, or whether it was merely a natural sound of bough or wind transformed into a voice by a high wrought imagination acting upon a sensitive nervous system, Arthur certainly regarded the occurrence as a supernatural warning. The interruption, whether supernatural or not, effected its purpose. The veil was torn from Arthur's eyes and he was again proof against temptation, however plausible and seductive. Once more he confirmed his resolve never to quit the path of duty, however difficult that path might be.

It is needless to say that Alicia possessed as high a sense of duty as he did. Neither would yield. Unfortunately the line of duty on the one side ran in exactly the opposite direction to the line of duty on the other, and so two hearts, which seemed destined at one time to coalesce, drifted apart. The proposal and the counter proposal had both been rejected. But each esteemed the other the more for sacrificing personal inclination, for sacrificing love, for sacrificing what appeared then, to both of them, a life's happiness, to duty.

Duty had triumphed, but at what an expense! Neither of them ever acknowledged, except perhaps in the inmost recess of his or her soul, that such a triumph went perilously near costing a broken heart.

* * * * * *

The next day the expected happened, for Arthur received a command from the Emperor to quit Altendorf and take up fresh quarters in Berlin, as certain work was required which necessitated his presence here for some time to come.

This was a great relief to both Alicia and Arthur; for, after the events of the preceding day, constant intercourse between them would have been painful.

When Arthur quitted the household of Von Lebenheim, many friendly expressions were used between host, hostess, and visitor, of regret on the one side and thanks on the other. And although several times subsequently, Arthur came in contact with Herr Von Lebenheim, he never again saw Alicia, except on one memorable occasion when he was again exposed to a terrible temptation—a temptation which was a thousand times more difficult to resist than the one which he encountered in the garden at Altendorf.

CHAPTER X.

IN WHICH THE PROPOSAL OF A HOME RULE BILL FOR ALSACE-LORRAINE CREATES A GREAT DEAL OF ASTONISHMENT.

SOON after the departure of Hardy from Altendorf for Berlin, the general public all over Europe were on the tip-toe of expectation. The morning paper on the breakfast table was each day opened in feverish anticipation that it would contain news of a declaration of war. Trade was almost at a standstill. The money market was awfully depressed. The uncertainty of what was going to happen affected securities to almost as great an extent as if war had been declared. The subordinate German Government officials who had charge of the measures for carrying out the provisions of the great Army Bill, were not only working night and day, but working, practically, as if war had already been declared. Mobilisation had been already carried on to an enormous extent, and vast numbers of soldiers and material of war were already encamped on both sides of the Franco-German frontier. The tension was almost at breaking point, and the world was wondering how it was that Germany had not declared war. For the impression was fast being firmly fixed in men's minds that Germany would, necessarily, take the offensive, and that consequently to Germany men's attention must be directed for the first move.

Just at this time there were certain disquieting rumours that there were dissensions in the German Government, and that some of the most prominent members were on the point of resigning. Then there were rumours that the Emperor was determined on a line of policy which was strongly opposed by his advisers. The wiseheads repudiated such rumours, and concluded that governmental dissensions at such a critical time would be sheer madness.

Rumours, however, were soon destined to be swallowed up by news of the most sensational character.

The German Premier had risen in the Reichstag and announced, amidst profound silence, his intention to introduce a Bill for

AMENDING THE CONSTITUTION AND GOVERNMENT
OF
ALSACE-LORRAINE.

So ran the innocent looking title of a Bill, which, if it ever became law, would have tremendous consequence for the German Empire. For this Bill embraced not only a comprehensive scheme of Home Rule for Alsace-Lorraine, but empowered the Executive of the Federal Government, should it be deemed advisable, to take a vote of all male residents of the provinces, over twenty-one years of age, in order to determine to what nationality these provinces should belong.

The Premier explained the various clauses of the proposed Bill; quoted the schedules annexed thereto;

mentioned the various safeguards which it was proposed to adopt in order to ensure that any elections under the Bill should be true and just elections; and gave the various contingencies which would warrant the holding of such elections. He gave a full explanation of every point touched upon by the measure without note or comment of his own; and then, in a few dignified sentences, announced that the measure he had alluded to was of such vast importance to the Empire, that he did not propose to ask the members of the Reichstag to discuss it then, but would take the earliest opportunity of asking the whole nation to give its opinion upon the momentous question. This meant the Dissolution of the Reichstag, and a General Election, to be held as soon as possible. The Premier then sat down amidst the same profound silence which had obtained during his speech. His announcement fairly took away the breath of his hearers. The secret had been well kept. No one, except those in the inner circle, knew what was coming, and the remaining members of the Reichstag were too profoundly moved by what they had heard, to emit those sounds which the reporters generally describe in brackets as (sensation).

Before the world was an hour older, details of the famous Home Rule scheme for the Alsatian provinces had been flashed over the telegraph wires to all the principal cities of the world.

To say that the news was received with sheer astonishment, is to use a very mild term where a much stronger one would be more applicable. The measure did not specify in so many words that Alsace-Lorraine would be handed voluntarily back again to France, but it distinctly paved the way for certain contingencies under which the residents might possibly elect that these provinces should belong to France and not to Germany. In fact, the ultimate decision whether Alsace-Lorraine should form part of one nation or the other, was referred to the inhabitants of these two provinces.

It was the first time that a Home Rule Bill was proposed which did not include safeguards against what is popularly termed " separatism."

For a day or two the majority of the German newspapers were too much horror-stricken to comment upon such a proposal. They confined themselves to a bare statement of the facts, and in the meantime employed all their ingenuity in ascertaining the genesis of the scheme. They quickly, however, recovered their self-possession, and then there burst over the country a perfect flood of press criticisms adverse to the scheme.

It very soon leaked out that the Emperor himself was responsible for launching the astounding proposals—nay, for forcing them upon his advisers. His high position, for once, was powerless to protect him from a shower of comments neither favourable nor complimentary. For once the press burst all restraints. With an outspoken freedom quite exceptional, the Emperor was called wilful, obstinate, headstrong; intoxicated with his own self-consciousness, hence blind to the best interests of the Empire! He was told that he had been so accustomed to have his wishes gratified that he had come to regard himself as an irresponsible autocrat.

He was reminded in no measured terms that he

had dabbled in politics once too often, and if he did not seriously reconsider his action, he would succeed in wrecking the Empire which his father and grandfather had, with so much courage and energy, built up. He was told to take an example by those limited monarchies, in which the sovereign ruled but did not attempt to govern. He was advised to avoid politics, and leave all questions of policy and details of government, to those who were best fitted for them— the Statesmen.

The Home Rule Scheme itself was exposed to a raking fire from all points. It was denounced as an attempt to disintegrate the Empire; to break down in a moment that which had cost thousands of lives, millions of treasure, and many years of anxious labour and preparation to build up. The scheme was described as an attempt to humiliate the nation, just at the very time when a glorious victory was in sight. Germany was told that by the proposal she voluntarily confessed herself weak, acknowledged her inferiority to France, and affirmed herself beaten by that power before a shot had been fired. It was declared that the army had received a dastardly insult added to a wanton injury.

It would be futile to attempt to enumerate the condemnatory adjectives which were employed; suffice it to say that the rich Teuton language was exhausted in finding words which adequately conveyed the various writers' horror and disgust at the bare proposal of such a drastic Home Rule Bill as this.

The Liberal as well as the extreme Radical newspapers and the Social Democratic party were all taken considerably aback. They knew not what to think. So different was the proposal from those which usually emanated from the Government, that they feared to applaud or even countenance the Bill. The project was certainly ultra-radical, and savoured of Socialism ;. and for this very reason they distrusted the Government. Had not the Government always been at mortal enmity with Socialism in general, and the Socialists in particular? Then might not the Bill hide some deep laid plot against Socialism? Might there not be some skilfully laid trap for the Socialists? If so, they would not walk into it with their eyes shut.

So the Liberal and Radical newspapers were inclined to hold their hands for a time.

Meantime the remainder of the press had it all their own way. Vested interests, militarism, the leading Conservatism of the age, and the Government departments, seemed to carry all before them in their energetic opposition to the Bill. The prevailing sentiment of the press was ably represented by one of the chief Conservative journals, in a leading article of which we herewith annex a portion. The article concluded as follows :

"We have endeavoured to discuss the preposterous scheme of Home Rule for Alsace-Lorraine with a certain degree of calmness ; but it is a scheme which bids defiance to calm discussion. The bare statement of what it proposes to do would excite laughter, if it did not provoke sadness. The Bill, without note or comment, emphatically condemns itself. Arguments are perfectly superfluous. Let us briefly summarise the situation. Here we have on the one hand a German nation, or rather combination of nations, united. Complete Germany is strong, never so strong as now. This strong Germany is seriously menaced by the hostile attitude of a neighbouring nation. This hostile attitude is developed until the situation becomes intolerable. By making enormous sacrifices, by passing an Army Bill of unparalleled stringency, and by other contingent measures, this strong and united Germany is in a state of preparedness for war surpassing anything hitherto imagined. A wonderful discovery in explosives has enormously increased the strength and preparedness of this already strong, prepared United Germany. It is now generally acknowledged what Queljanite implies and what it can do for Germany. A German army, possessed with a sufficient quantity of this deadly explosive, can absolutely obliterate any opposing force or combination of forces. At this juncture there is launched from the German Reichstag a Bill which, disguise it as we may, proposes to hand over Alsace-Lorraine to France ; to the very country which at the present moment is straining to fly at the throat of Germany. At one stroke, strong, prepared United Germany is acknowledged weak, unequipped, disintegrated ; our foe has gained a brilliant victory ; and we hand over the honours of war to France.

"The German Confederation may be likened to a vessel of toughened glass. This is homogeneous and will resist blows only up to a certain point. Once past this critical point, molecular change is very sudden and complete. The vessel shivers into a thousand fragments. So with the German Confederation. It is united and compact, and will resist disintegrating tension up to a certain point. Let the tension be carried beyond this point and the Confederation crumbles to pieces. But we are told that the nation will be asked for its direct opinion upon this Bill. Granted! But suppose for the sake of argument that the dissolution has taken place, the general election has been held, and the Bill emphatically rejected. Think you that Germany will emerge as strong, as prepared, and as united as before? No! The Bill will be dead, but Germany will long feel the disintegrating and weakening effect of the whole business. Let us hope, in the best interest of a united, prepared, and strong Germany, that we have already heard the last of the Bill for handing over the Alsatian provinces to France, misnamed the Bill for Amending the Constitution and Government of Alsace-Lorraine."

CHAPTER XI.

SHOWING HOW "MARMADUKE" ISSUES A MANIFESTO, AND THE EFFECT IT HAS UPON VARIOUS CLASSES OF SOCIETY.

IT is needless to say that the conception of such a bold stroke as Home Rule for Alsace-Lorraine, and such complete Home Rule, was due to the fertile brain of that idealist dreamer, Arthur Hardy; who must henceforth be designated by his adopted *nom-de-plume* " Marmaduke." But to the indomitable will and energy of the Emperor belonged the credit of translating that conception into action and forcing upon a reluctant Government the task of launching the scheme.

It will never be known whether the Emperor originally intended that any other personality but his own should appear in connection with the matter. Suffice it to say that when the press overflowed with indignation and opposition, and demanded the immediate withdrawal of the obnoxious Bill, an attempt was made to compel our friend Hardy to adopt the *rôle* of political scapegoat. For the word was passed quietly round in the form of a rumour (probably inspired by some member of the Government) which rumour soon permeated every strata of society, that the mysterious " Marmaduke " was really the responsible influence; that the much-dreaded

Socialist revolution was at hand, and that a reign of terror and anarchy was imminent.

The authors of this rumour, however, in making their calculations, had omitted to take into account two important factors. One was the irrepressible enthusiasm of the social reformer; the other was the iron will of an Emperor who believed that he embodied in his person the providence of his country.

The storm of opposition was at its height when the following manifesto appeared over the signature " Marmaduke " :

"TO THE GERMAN NATION.

" A crisis has arrived in your career. Take heed, therefore, how you act.

" There is no disguising the fact that if the ' Bill for Amending the Constitution and Government of Alsace-Lorraine ' becomes law, these provinces will be asked to declare whether they will elect to belong to Germany or to France. If they reply ' Germany ' then, naturally, you will hold them against the world. If, on the other hand, they reply ' France,' you will allow them to embrace the opportunity of once more belonging to that nation.

" The practical outcome, however, of the whole matter remains the same. Germany makes a voluntary proposal of peace and goodwill towards France.

" The form in which the proposal is made is certainly startling. Let us examine the situation. Is such a course advantageous for Germany

I say, Yes! Posterity will echo, Yes! Does it constitute a dismemberment or disintegration of the German empire? I say, No! Posterity will echo, No!

"Let us consider.

"To make a voluntary offer of the recession of provinces which have been forcibly taken and forcibly held is but an act of justice, of restitution, and therefore of conciliation.

"Millions have been spent in transforming these provinces into a huge camp, a huge fortress. Does not this fact convey its own moral?

"We are face to face with a startling innovation. It is not proposed to treat the subject provinces as pawns on a chess-board. They are to elect their own destiny. Here righteousness and justice supersede custom and precedent. Imagine the proposal carried out. Imagine Alsace-Lorraine crying out with one voice, 'Let us belong to France.' Imagine the recession made. Where will you find warmer friends and greater supporters of Germany than in the two provinces? Did a policy of righteousness and justice ever disintegrate a nation? On the contrary, such a proposal as you have before you will succeed in uniting and consolidating the empire to a degree hitherto unthought.

"Again, does such a proposal indicate that Germany acknowledges her inferiority to France? I say, No! Are you not powerful? Is not your army the strongest in Europe? Do not your new explosives render you practically invulnerable, and place you far and away superior to any other army or combination of armies? Then you can afford—nay, you are the only Continental military nation which can afford—to be just, which can afford to be generous. For you are absolutely above suspicion. Such a course of action, under such circumstances, is more than advantageous: it is a paramount necessity. It is more than generous: it is godlike.

"What will be the result? Once the main cause of irritation between Germany and France removed, and removed in such a manner, cordial friendship between these two powerful nations must ensue. When generosity and conciliation shake hands, an alliance must follow. What is the consequence? The balance of power for the next century lies in the hands of a United Germany and France; the complexion of Europe changes, and we are within measurable distance of a general and material reduction in European armaments.

"With disarmament, even partial, Europe awakes from that horrible nightmare of impending war, from which she has suffered so long; taxation is reduced, commerce is no longer stifled, and the people can once more turn their thoughts to the peaceful arts.

"Many social and political customs, precedents, and systems have been tried for centuries. To your sorrow you have found them wanting. Rumour says that a social revolution is impending. Quite true. But it will be a bloodless revolution; a beneficent revolution; a revolution which is intended to cleanse the land of the foul weeds of class and national hatred ; a revolution which will prepare the ground for the good growths of love, peace, and prosperity. This revolution is inevitable and imminent. But you will have no reason to dread it. On the contrary you will welcome it. For this revolution is nothing more nor less than a rebirth of Christianity. The old world standards of thought and action are destined to pass away. You know it. Let your nation be one of the first to adopt the new standard, the standard of righteousness, justice, and peace, which in the future must be the supreme factors in all national and political, as in all social and commercial questions.

"Again—you are not asked to have something done for you. You are asked to do it yourselves, in a perfectly legitimate and constitutional manner. You have burdens ? Then lift those burdens from your own shoulders.

"It is for you to say :

> "Whether the golden rule shall be applied to questions of Imperial Policy.
>
> "Whether peace and goodwill shall supersede the rule of ' Blood and Iron.'
>
> "Whether the ' good old rule, the simple plan, that they shall take who have the power, and they shall keep who can,' shall be declared obsolete.
>
> "Whether an attempt shall be made to settle international disputes by a more advantageous method than the suicidal one of war.

"Whether a nation, which for centuries has called itself Christian, shall apply Christian principles to its politics and its diplomacy.

"Are you patriotic? Have you ambition that succeeding generations shall point to the German Empire as the apotheosis of civilised development? Then help to make your country the foremost in the world for righteousness and justice.

"Remember that righteousness and justice not only exalt a nation, but sustain it when it is exalted.

"Has the 'Imperial Idea' a charm for you? Then develop and extend the true 'Imperial Idea' by advancing one step nearer to that grandest of all Imperial Ideas, The Brotherhood of Man and the Federation of the World.

"Have you chivalry? Then support your beloved Emperor in his heroic attempt to become the foremost champion of right in Europe.

"Would you be mighty? Then remember that the nation which aspires to be a mighty conqueror in the world's battle, will be the one which conquers war, which conquers wrong, which conquers hatred, which conquers injustice, which conquers oppression, which conquers revenge, which conquers selfishness.

"Let the great German nation be that mighty conqueror.

"You say you have no precedents. Then make one.

"Europe is in a state of flux. Be yours the noble task to supply the matrix.

"Do the right and mould Europe!

"MARMADUKE."

*　　*　　*　　*　　*　　*

Have you ever witnessed, reader, the beautiful process of crystallisation? There is a saturated solution of some salt, all is ready, molecular tension is great. But the solution remains clear, no crystals are visible. Suddenly a point is reached when the molecular strain is overcome. Minute spicules form, the delicate tracery of crystals silently appears. That which was not is, and beautiful geometric figures fill the solution.

So with the manifesto. Social and political tension was enormous. The world was ready for the introduction of a new social and political system. But a starting point was necessary; that point was provided by the manifesto, and round it crystallised new thoughts, new hopes, new aspirations.

No new truth was disclosed in this manifesto. The principles it spoke of were old and familiar to everybody. But it directed men's thoughts into new and strange applications of those old truths.

The world was sick to death of war national, of war social, of war commercial, of war of every kind; but the world considered war, militarism, and their dread concomitants, inevitable.

The manifesto appeared; the psychological moment arrived. Then came a glimmer of light and a glimmer of hope. The downtrodden masses caught the idea. The Socialists caught the idea. The common people read the manifesto gladly, as nineteen centuries before the common people heard Christ gladly, and for the same reasons. Needless to say the annexed provinces were ablaze from one end to the other with the old French sentiment, and Alsace-Lorraine was fairly frantic with joy and hope.

The manifesto raised enthusiasm where previously reigned apathy.

Another strange thing happened. Within the last few years woman had been coming more and more to the front; quietly, unobtrusively, but effectually. The manifesto appeared. Then woman spake out and threw in the weight of her influence with Marmaduke and his manifesto.

All great politico-international questions had hitherto turned upon the strength and power, military and naval, of certain nations and combinations of nations; and the map of the world had been constructed accordingly.

Hitherto brute force had been recognised as the final arbiter in human affairs.

A new force, or set of forces, was about to be introduced. Would these new forces conquer the world? If not, there was nothing before the world but a policy of black despair.

It is needless to say that officialdom and bureaucracy were dead against the Bill and the manifesto. Vested interests, when attacked, not only die hard, but rally around them those other sympathetic vested interests which are not directly attacked; and the whole resist progress to the death.

This was probably the reason why (leaving out the Radical and Socialist newspapers) the manifesto appeared to have very slight influence upon the

German press. The main portion of the press, with very few exceptions, had been captured so completely by the influence of militarism, the influence of privilege, the influence of conservatism, the influence of prejudice, the influence of a spurious imperialism; that the opposition of the press to both the Bill and the manifesto was overwhelming. The great majority of the newspapers declared that they led public opinion, and that they reflected public opinion. The general election soon to take place would prove whether this majority was right or wrong.

CHAPTER XII.

HOW SOME OF THE TEACHERS AND PREACHERS OF RELIGION RECEIVED THE MANIFESTO. A PYRRHIC VICTORY!

THE arguments in Marmaduke's manifesto were founded on a religious basis. They spoke of righteousness and justice. They spoke of a re-birth of Christianity and the application of Christian principles to high political questions. What did the religious teachers and preachers of Germany, those whose special province it was to instruct the people in the tenets of Christianity, the Christian guides of the nation, the prelates and the clergy, the leaders of those churches which, whether strictly national or not, whether possessing State recognition or not, were nevertheless regarded as entitled to speak on behalf of their respective churches, have to say on the subject?

It is sad to be obliged to record the fact that a large number opposed the Bill and ignored the manifesto.

What! Teachers of Christianity ignore an appeal to exactly those Christian principles which it was their special province to inculcate? What! The teachers of Christianity on the side of militarism, class ascendency, privilege, prejudice, injustice, unrighteousness? Strange, but true.

How is this? Let us consider.

Nineteen hundred years ago the distinguishing characteristics of the most highly developed national religion in the world—the Jewish religion—were ritualism, clericalism, priestism, dogmatism. And it was exactly these characteristics, as opposed to the spirit of true religion, which prompted the Jewish clergy to reject Christianity and murder Christ.

Nineteen hundred years have elapsed, and we find many religious teachers exhibiting much the same characteristics. Strange that nineteen hundred years of Christianity have made such little impression upon theological and ecclesiastical misconceptions!

Take the religious history of the latter part of the last decade of the nineteenth, and the earlier portion of the first decade of the twentieth century. What do we find? The tide of reaction rising.

A combination of circumstances—militarism in some countries, religious apathy in others, a false security in some—had apparently conspired to arrest the progress of religious liberty.

Taking full advantage of this combination of circumstances, inch by inch, bit by bit, slowly but surely, the claims of the dogmatist, the cleric, the ritualist, the priest, were pushed forward.

Inch by inch, bit by bit, clericalism sought once more to regain its supremacy.

Look where you would, the result was the same. You saw churches belonging to different nationalities, under different circumstances, in different ways, all working independently of each other, but all working in the same direction and to the same end.

Apparently clericalism had gained a triumph,

more or less pronounced, all along the line. Then became visible the direct result. Dissent from clericalism was sternly repressed in some countries; was harshly persecuted in others, where it could not be absolutely crushed; and was rendered distinctly unfashionable, where it could not be persecuted.

Given a State-supported church, with, of necessity, its dignitaries, its predominance, and its privileges; sooner or later we are certain to find clustering around it religious subject races. And wherever we find religious subject races, we have not far to seek for oppression and injustice.

In Protestant England the tide of Ritualism rose higher and higher. The exodus of young people from the narrow and sober paths of Dissent to the broad and agreeable way of Ritualistic episcopalianism was already provoking comment. The Evangelical and Broad Church parties became mere names, memories, histories, rather than actualities. There was no common action between the High Church party and the Roman Catholic Church, but it was noticed that, coincident with the upward progress of the former, the accessions to the latter were enormous. If Ritualism and Roman Catholicism had not practically captured religious England, they had certainly strengthened their position to an enormous extent.

Spain, Italy, and France had long been lying prostrate under the feet of a dogmatic Roman Catholicism, and latterly the bands had been tightened and the victims more firmly held.

The Orthodox Church had succeeded in tying Russia hand and foot; and, moreover, tied her in a manner distinctly brutal.

In all countries the same reactionary powers had sought to gag and bind and wind round and round with the cerements of the grave, the beautiful living palpitating Christianity.

In Russia, the Orthodox Church, sure of the phlegmatic Great Russians, was making superhuman efforts to prevent the Germanised Little Russians escaping from their religious bonds. The tortures of the Middle Ages, and the resources of a later civilisation and irresponsible autocracy were all employed in a frantic endeavour to crush religious freedom.

In countries which had not the advantages of an unlimited use of the knout, the Cossack, and Siberia, an effort for religious freedom meant the stigma of irreligion, atheism, secularism. In some cases this stigma was deserved ; for a people disgusted with the spurious Christianity presented to them, rejected all Christianity and all religion.

In most cases freedom of religious thought, if it wished to exist at all, had to exist outside the national churches.

In Germany the conditions were not identical with those of other countries, Whilst the German constitution provided for entire liberty of conscience and for complete social equality amongst all religious confessions, the relation between Church and State varied in the different States of the Empire.

Still, notwithstanding varying conditions, the aspect of the religious question was pretty much the same in Germany as elsewhere. Roman Catholicism, whether in Germany or any other country, wore much the same complexion and developed in much the same manner. The reformed German Lutheran Church, whatever it may once have been, was now hardly to be distinguished from its Roman Catholic neighbour. The one gave allegiance to the Pope, the other did not. The forms and ceremonies of one differed from the forms and ceremonies of the other. But so far as dogmatic ecclesiasticism and departure from the Christianity of Christ was concerned, the two Churches might be regarded as twin sisters.

Religious reaction was quite as apparent in Germany as other countries.

Had sacerdotalism indeed won a great victory? It appeared so. But it was a Pyrrhic victory! Like Napoleon when he marched into Moscow, what seemed a triumphant conclusion to a brilliant campaign proved the beginning of disaster.

Christianity was not dead simply because it was bound for burial.

When Marmaduke's manifesto appeared, the German nation was ready (as, indeed, other nations were ready) for a great religious revolt—a revolt against dogma, against clericalism, against priestism, against religiosity, against reaction. The world was ripe for taking Christ as the true arbitrator in social and commercial as well as in international disputes; for allowing His spirit to soften the asperities of life; His principles to be applied to diplomacy and commerce.

Christianity, despite the efforts and apparent success of the foes within its own household, had progressed and developed. Like all great developments, its progress, which had been gradual, now became catastrophic. The time had come and the man had appeared. The spirit of Christianity, as if by magic, at the touch of Marmaduke, broke through the crust of ecclesiasticism which had enveloped it, and began to flow in all directions.

The millions who had been offered a stone, now demanded bread, and there sprang into existence at one bound a great religious revolt—a revolt which, in conjunction with a coincident social revolt, threatened to overthrow priestism and to overthrow militarism ; in other words, to overthrow oppression, spiritual and physical.

The leaders, the prelates, the large majority of the clergy, instinctively felt that this great revolt was as much against them and their teaching as against existing social conditions. Therefore they bitterly opposed the Bill and studiously ignored the manifesto.

Marmaduke's words were indeed coming true. The re-birth of Christianity was taking place.

CHAPTER XIII.

A BOLT FROM THE BLUE. A DIABOLICAL OUTRAGE THREATENS TO PUT BACK THE CLOCK OF PROGRESS MANY YEARS.

THE Emperor's action, added to the manifesto, bid fair to bring those two extreme wings in German politics—the sovereign and the ultra Radicals—into line. A fusion of the extreme Socialists with monarchy meant a Germany more united than many people dared hope.

But the enemies of peace and progress had by no means given up the contest. Help to the opponents of the Bill came from an unexpected source.

Directly after the manifesto appeared, the Emperor received numerous addresses from various sections of the community who rejoiced at his proposal regarding Alsace-Lorraine, and promised him their loyal support in translating the proposal into action. Amongst them was one from the Socialists of the capital, and arrangements had been made that a rather large deputation should be allowed to present this address to the Kaiser, at his imperial palace in Berlin, in the new wing which had recently been remodelled and rebuilt.

At the time appointed, this deputation, consisting of about 120 representatives of the Socialism of

Berlin, were admitted to the inner courtyard of the palace.

The Emperor appeared on a balcony overlooking the courtyard. Three of the chosen representatives were conducted to this balcony. The remainder of the deputation viewed the proceedings from the courtyard beneath.

It was a beautiful afternoon. The sun shone upon the scene as well as in the hearts of those present. The occasion was a joyful one for all. The address had been duly read by one of the three favoured representatives. The Emperor had stepped forward to the front of the balcony, and was in the midst of a spirited speech, partly read from notes which he held in his hand, and partly delivered extempore; when a dark-coloured missile, rather larger than an orange, was suddenly thrown from the back of the group beneath, straight towards the Emperor. He did not see it, but those standing near him did, and instinctively fell back.

Everyone knew in a moment it was a bomb! Just as it was about to strike its object, a pale-faced, slight form was seen to dash forwards, stretch forth his right hand, and dexterously catch the bomb. It was Marmaduke who had saved the Emperor. The horror-stricken spectators had not time to give a sigh of relief at this wonderful escape, when a second bomb was similarly thrown in the same direction. This was caught by Marmaduke in his left hand. Immediately afterwards came a third bomb. Whether excitement had finally unnerved the hand which threw the bombs, or whether the aim was diverted in some other way, the last missile, although evidently thrown with great force, fell considerably short of its mark, and struck a column supporting the balcony. Instantly a vivid flash and a deafening explosion took place. Small nails, with which the bomb had been packed, rained upon the upturned heads of the deputation, and fragments of iron, pieces of the bomb itself, were scattered in all directions. The heavy stone balcony had efficiently protected the Emperor and those who were standing with him. But the scene below was fearful.

Blood streamed from those who had been struck. Groans and screams filled the air. The scene was one of indescribable horror and confusion. The Emperor, however, kept his head, and immediately in a loud voice ordered the outer gates to be closed and guarded to prevent the escape of anyone. Marmaduke also kept his head, and still retained undamaged in his hands the two bombs he had so courageously and skilfully caught. For, by one of those strange scientific freaks so common where explosives are concerned, the almost inevitable "sympathetic explosion" of the bombs held by Marmaduke had not taken place.

Discipline and order soon prevailed; attendants and others inside the palace hurried to the spot, and the wounded were soon receiving every attention.

It was found that scarcely a single person who had stood in the courtyard escaped injury. The fact of their faces being upturned at the time, and the bomb exploding immediately above them, caused most of the injuries to be received on the head and face. No one was actually killed outright, but numerous sufferers sustained terrible fractures of the skull; the faces of many were shattered to pieces, and scores were blinded for life. Whilst the mangled victims were being cared for, the search for the perpetrator was carried on. He was soon found. In fact, he boasted of the deed, and only regretted that the Emperor and those who surrounded him were not blown to pieces.

The name of the miscreant was Schwartz, well known as a violent, noisy, self-assertive, frothy Anarchist. He had only sustained a few trifling cuts, and was quickly taken to prison.

Of course the deed was deprecated by the whole of the press. All newspapers, and all persons, except the small violent section of irreconcilables, united in congratulating the Emperor on his escape, and denouncing the diabolical outrage. None were more prompt with congratulations and denunciations, none were more ready to acknowledge the suicidal policy of such a deed, than the Liberal, Radical, and Socialist sections.

But, at the same time, the opposition was not slow to take political advantage of the affair. They tried to connect the outrage with Socialist organisations. They said to their supporters, "We told you so. This outrage is the direct result of pandering to Socialism. In Socialism—or what amounts to the same thing, Anarchism—the Emperor is nourishing a viper in his bosom. It has tried to fasten its poisonous fangs in his flesh. Let him tear the noxious reptile from his breast and crush it under foot, ere it has time and opportunity to make another, and, possibly, more successful attempt.

"Happily the Socialists have been hoist with their

own petard, actually, as well as metaphorically. Let us hope that we have heard the last of mad Socialists and their mad schemes."

It is curious to note what a strange similarity sometimes exists between certain things which outwardly and apparently are perfectly dissimilar.

Militarism would indignantly repudiate any connection or similarity, however remote, with anarchy. Public opinion places them as far asunder as the poles. To the one is attached the title of "honorable profession of arms"; to the other is applied epithets of opprobrium and reproach. One marches proudly in broad daylight with music and flags, the other slinks in the hidden darkness. With one is connected glory and honour, with the other disgrace and degradation.

Analyse results, however, and what do we find?

They are both the visible embodiment of brute force. Neither of them has the slightest regard or pity for their innocent victims. They are both engaged in ringing the terrible changes on suffering, death, and disaster. They are each the antitheses of right. They are each absolutely void of utility or benefit. They are each the sworn enemies to progress, justice, or righteousness. Nations have progressed in spite of, not in consequence of, either militarism or anarchism.

Does war produce anything but national chaos? Is anarchism intended to produce anything but social chaos? Granted that one chaos is on a smaller scale than the other, yet it is still chaos.

Whatever satisfaction could be legitimately and decently expressed, was expressed by the opposition at this juncture—satisfaction, not at the outrage itself, not at the work of the outrage mongers; but satisfaction at the possible result, namely, the crushing of the hopes of the friends of progress.

Militarism and anarchism had indeed joined forces, and were both working to the same end.

When it was known that it was the hand of Marmaduke which had saved the Emperor, and that this mysterious Marmaduke was really a person, and not a hazy, indefinite organisation, the general interest regarding him was increased. The people were eager to see him; and there could be no doubt that had he chosen to publicly drive through the streets of Berlin, or in fact, of any other German town, he would have been received by the populace with enthusiasm and delight. But he was still unwilling to emerge from his seclusion. The Emperor pressed him. Marmaduke responded by asking a boon. It was that he should receive no honours and should not be urged to parade himself before the public, at any rate at present. His wish was granted.

Meanwhile, congratulations were literally showered upon the Emperor. The Municipality of Berlin, as well as that of other cities, the Federal Council, members of the Reichstag, members of the Prussian Diet and other subsidiary governments, local bodies, political bodies, commercial boards, as well as private individuals, vied with each other in showing their delight at their Kaiser's extraordinary escape.

These congratulations were too numerous to be replied to individually, so the Emperor caused a characteristic letter of thanks to be published to the following effect:—

"TO MY GERMAN PEOPLE.

" I am touched by the warmth of affection which you have shown, in the numerous addresses and letters of congratulation upon my escape from a horrible death. I thank you all from the bottom of my heart.

" I shall always retain a vivid impression of such attachment. I ask you to join with me in most sincerely thanking Divine Providence for that special interposition by which I am still preserved in that exalted position in which it has pleased Almighty God to place me.

"The untoward event shall not deter me from continuing, during the remainder of my life, so miraculously preserved, that line of policy, which I have always followed, a policy which has for its sole object the promotion of the safety, honour, and welfare of the great Empire of which I am the head.

"It must not be forgotten that our thanks are also due to the instrument of Divine Providence; that noble hand which arrested the progress of the murderous bombs. The act shall never be forgotten by me.

(Signed) "WILHELM."

The trial of Schwartz, the Anarchist, duly took place. The case against him was so clear that, despite the efforts of his advocate, he was sentenced to death.

The death penalty, however, was never carried out. The Emperor declared that Anarchists were madmen and should be treated as such. By an exercise of the Imperial clemency, therefore, the sentence was commuted to incarceration for life in a lunatic asylum.

The Reichstag, moreover, did not commit the blunder of legislating in a panic. They now recognised, what indeed should have been apparent all along, that a militant Anarchist was a violent madman, and his treatment should be neither more nor less severe than that which was merited by a dangerous lunatic.

CHAPTER XIV.

ELECTIONEERING EXCITEMENT. THE BATTLE OF THE BALLOT-BOX AND THE RESULT THEREOF.

IT is needless to say that intense excitement prevailed throughout Germany. A general election, even in the quietest of times, always raises the political temperature. The state of nervous tension may be imagined, therefore, when such burning topics as the Home Rule Bill and all that it involved were on the carpet.

It was now the 10th of June, and the 13th had been fixed for holding the general Parliamentary elections throughout Germany.

No practical alterations had been made within recent years in the mode or conditions of election.

As everyone knows, the Reichstag or Imperial Parliament consists of 397 members. Election is by universal suffrage and direct secret ballot. The elections are held on one day, and the elected candidate must have an absolute majority of votes; so that in case of more than two candidates, should the highest not poll more than the aggregate of all his rivals, the two highest scorers must undergo another election, which is generally held within a fortnight of the first. Although by the Constitution popular representation exists, the Government has the absolute right of veto.

Marmaduke prophesied in his manifesto that the startling proposal before the country would have the effect of uniting rather than disintegrating the nation, and this prophesy was already in process of fulfilment. For, at previous general elections, the multiplicity of parties was astounding, and the electors had thrust before them the claims of Old Conservatives, Free Conservatives, National Liberals, Liberal Unionists, Liberal Democrats, South German Democrats, Social Democrats, Clericals, Anti-semite Poles, Guelphs, Danes, Alsace-Lorrainers, not to mention Agrarians, Non-Agrarians, Protestants, Free Traders, Bimetallists, Fifth Monarchy Men, and many others, all of whom hoped to pull something out of the political pot.

But in view of the grave issues before them, each candidate was forced to put in the forefront of his candidature " I am for, or against, the Bill." For once, minor differences, sectional party passions, and collateral issues melted away, and Germany was united—for or against the Bill.

It was the eve of the elections, yet it was impossible to foretell the result. Anyone who read the newspapers would still be struck with the preponderance of opposition to the Bill. At the same time indications were not wanting that the masses were veering round in favour of the Bill. In previous struggles in the Imperial Parliament, the balance of parties had been the Emperor, the Government, and the Conservatives *versus* the Social Democratic and kindred elements ; and the Emperor and the Government generally carried the day. Now new combinations came into existence, and it was the Emperor *plus* the Proletariat *versus* the bureaucratic and privileged classes.

What would be the result of the new combination? Even now the national sentiment in favour of holding the captured provinces at any cost, might have wrecked any attempt to force a Home Rule Bill for Alsace-Lorraine through Parliament, had it not been for that great and growing grievance, the military system.

Militarism was one of the most terrible foes to progress the world had ever seen. Not only was the flower of Europe abstracted from productive work, but additional burdens were thrown on the weak and those who remained, to support the strong and commercially-idle soldier. Trade was paralysed, and social misery was the result.

A significant fact may be here mentioned. The Emperor had occasion to drive through the crowded streets of the city in an open carriage during the dinner hour. He was vociferously cheered by thousands of the people, whose enthusiasm knew no bounds. The same evening he attended a special representation at the opera, when prices were doubled, and the audience almost exclusively composed of the upper classes. The Emperor was received with a most chilling silence.

It is a recognised fact, however, that journalistic comments, enthusiasm in the streets, and cheers at election meetings cannot always foreshadow the verdict of the ballot-box; so on this eve of the great election the excitement was intense, for no one knew what the result would be.

  * * * * * *

The 13th of June had passed and the first elections were over. The public read the published results with feverish anxiety. Of the 397 elections there was only an absolute majority in 183. Of these it was known that 110 elected candidates were in favour of the Bill and 73 against. The advanced Liberal and Social Democratic elements had won all along the line. In the first elections the Emperor and his coadjutor, "Marmaduke," were victorious.

For once the majority of the newspapers were wrong.

For once they had not led public opinion; they had not even reflected it.

There still remained, however, 214 elections to account for, and those elections might turn the scale either way.

Excitement increased. If there were excitement over the first elections, this was multiplied tenfold as the time for the second or test elections arrived. The Social Democrats were jubilant. They saw the dawning of the day of emancipation from the thraldom of detested systems. This filled them with fresh vigour. They redoubled their exertions. They were simply frantic with excited enthusiasm. Marmaduke's manifesto was the rallying point and the battle cry. Round it the hosts contended. Marmaduke, true to his instinct, was still to a great extent the mysterious. He had never made himself visible during the elections. Pressure had been brought to bear upon him in a very high quarter to make himself known to the populace. He was firm in his refusal, and for the present he was right. Mystery and truth had joined hands, and the combined influence of a mysterious ideal and his manifesto, breathing righteousness and enthusiasm in every line, was far greater than the influence of a mere visible person. In the first elections to a great, but in the second elections, to a far greater extent, " Marmaduke " was the name to conjure with. As the days advanced, the manifesto bore more fruit. Principles were talked about more than policy or results. It began to be felt that Marmaduke, besides being on the winning side, was right. It was felt that principles and the application of those principles should come first, and that mere results could safely be left to take care of themselves. For, if once principles and their application were decided on a basis of right, it was impossible for the results to be wrong.

So, amid scenes of excitement absolutely unparalleled in the country, the test elections were held.

* * * * * *

They were all over and the results were known. Of the 214 supplementary elections, 120 had been gained by candidates favourable to the Bill, 89 by those opposed to the Bill, and 5 by men who sat on the fence. So that, giving the uncertain votes to the opposition, the Emperor and Marmaduke held 230 votes, and opposed to them were 167 votes, a majority for the Home Rule Bill of 63.

Of course the Bill had to pass its various readings. It had to become law and it had to be put into force. But, for good or ill, the result was regarded as a foregone conclusion.

Militarism had received a great blow, the greatest blow which had ever been directed against it.

Undoubtedly the greatest triumph of the new order consisted in the fact that peace counsels had prevailed, notwithstanding the existence of such a potent force for evil and destruction as Queljanite ; and notwithstanding the hindrance which had been caused by the Anarchist outrage.

Marmaduke's words, when he held that memorable first conversation with the Emperor at the German Embassy in London, had come true.

Germany had again triumphed over her hereditary foe. But the triumph was one of peace, not of war. Germany was again the victor, but the victory was due to love and generosity, not to arms and bloodshed.

The great ship of the German Empire had pursued its even course for many years; it had weathered storms and escaped shoals. It was now about to alter its course many points. Unknown rocks were to be encountered, unknown waters navigated. Would it reach the promised haven in safety, and would it be able to lay down a chart which should guide the other good ships of Europe to the same haven?

CHAPTER XV.

RELATES SOME OF THE MOTIVES WHICH ACTUATED THE POLICY OF THE GERMAN EMPEROR.

THE reader may have considered it absurd, nay incredible, that the German Emperor, a sovereign who for so many years so closely identified himself with militarism, should have suddenly turned right round and apparently stultified himself by listening to, much less carrying out, any suggestions which would practically effect the overthrow of military supremacy.

But the Emperor was perfectly consistent in all he did. Further, not only did he carry out a policy of harmonious continuity, but exhibited remarkable astuteness in regard to that policy, as we shall presently see.

The German Emperor was a born leader, a born sovereign. Further, he considered that he governed by divine right and was consequently under the direct protection of the Almighty. He accepted this position as a matter of course, and considered it was his simple duty to uphold such a position in all its integrity. That being so, it goes without saying that he considered his will was paramount, as the will of the viceregent of the Almighty should be. Consequently he possessed an iron will without knowing it; at any rate he was able to exercise his iron will without the slightest expenditure of mental exertion. With this heaven-given position as Emperor, was interwoven his position as head of the army. The one was a perfect complement of the other. He considered he was the personal embodiment of German Imperialism, as well as of German Militarism. So long as the military idea predominated, *he* was the military idea.

It is true that the Emperor saw before him a horrible chaos of militarism, a possible reign of terror, and an impending social convulsion. He felt that he was being driven by events as they occurred, and he knew not from day to day in what direction those events would take either him or his country.

But he also felt that his only strength was in the army; his only safeguard was in militarism. The army, and the army only, could save the country.

Then there came a revelation to him. Marmaduke appeared on the scene. This strange individual reduced chaos to order. He showed the Emperor exactly the direction in which the combination of forces was leading the country. He mapped out the present situation and then plotted out another and an ideal future situation. Bit by bit he constructed out of the old order a new order. Side by side he built up the future of the old system and the future of the new. So clearly and so logically did Marmaduke present these two alternative futures, that the Emperor recognised that he had to deal with something more than a mere social reformer—a veritable social and political prophet.

Marmaduke was opposed to autocratic government. But he recognised that a democracy could be autocratic as well as an Emperor. Therefore, he was not one of that numerous body of Socialists who believed that the abolition of the monarchical principle was a necessary prelude to the regeneration of society.

He did not propose to pull down and destroy existing institutions, to reduce society to anarchy, in order to build up some impossible Utopia. He took society as he found it ; then remodelled, regenerated, and reformed it in harmony with the natural progress and development of the new order.

The Socialists' Utopia was impracticable; Marmaduke's proposals were practical. Hence the Emperor could listen to Marmaduke, when he could not listen to the many wild schemes of the Socialists.

Once the Emperor's mind was fully prepared for the reception of these new ideas, it did not take him long to perceive that ultimately militarism would have to give place to a newer and more powerful force. From the moment he saw that such a transference of forces was inevitable, he could find no reason against, but every reason in favour of this transference being effected by and through him.

He was perfectly well aware that armaments had been and were increasing, and that militarism was never so strong as now, but he was equally well aware that this fact could not prevent a development that was inevitable.

When the Emperor fully appreciated this revelation, he considered it the most natural thing in the world that a new system should supplant an old one, and further considered that he was the only fit and proper person to effect this operation, so far as Germany was concerned. In fact, he considered that his divine right as sovereign was actually confirmed by what appeared a special interposition of Providence, which enabled him to read the future and lead the nation from the old paths to the new.

He fully agreed in mind with Bacon's warning in his famous "Essay on Innovations," that "they who will not adopt new remedies must look out for new evils."

Carlyle would have praised him, for he was one of those who "argue not with the inexorable."

But the Emperor was actuated by another motive. Now that his eyes had been opened, he saw that sovereigns, ministers, governments, and diplomatists had carried militarism too far. The military Frankenstein was getting beyond the control of those who had brought it into existence. This monster was devouring the people right and left. A fearful revolt against its cruelties and excesses was inevitable, and the Emperor required no great astuteness to recognise that the bloody social reign which must ensue, would strike a death-dealing blow at imperialism and cause the downfall of many dynasties.

He was very jealous of his order, and was, therefore, resolved to give battle to the devastating Frankenstein, prevent the impending revolution, and save imperialism in general and his own dynasty in particular.

But even if a violent revolution did not suddenly deprive all sovereigns of their thrones, he could foresee that the only stable sovereigns of the future would be those who recognised that the inevitable trend of progress was decidedly in the direction of "government of the people, for the people, by the people."

He also knew that a republican government was not invariably an unmixed blessing; that democracy, as well as sovereignty, could be autocratic.

Here, then, was a good opportunity to take time by the forelock, help natural progress, and show his fellow monarchs how to direct popular government, so that a new lease of life might be given to the principle of sovereignty.

Another probable actuating motive must not be lost sight of.

The Emperor had inherited his position. He had not won it. He was not a mighty conqueror, but he doubtless aspired to be one; so that he was quite as willing to yoke his car to righteousness as to militarism, provided it carried him on to victory.

He was the first European sovereign who was both able and willing to become a mighty leader and a mighty conqueror in the new order. Nearly all great victories have been won by downright pluck; and, certainly without knowing it, pluck the Emperor possessed to an extraordinary degree. After all, it is only the first step which costs, and the Emperor took that step.

We have said that the Emperor recognised in Marmaduke a veritable prophet. But how if this prophet should prove a rival? A rival would never be tolerated where an instrument would be welcome. Marmaduke, however, never evinced the slightest ambition to shine as a great man, or to exert any influence but a moral influence. Officialdom had no charms for him. Therefore, the interests of the two never clashed, but most harmoniously dovetailed together.

Such were the relations between the Emperor and Marmaduke when they first met, and such were the relations which continued to exist between them.

Marmaduke occupied no official position whatever. Honours had been offered to him, both in consideration of his intrepid conduct in saving the life of the Emperor, and in suggesting a policy which, successful or not, at any rate was being adopted. But honours of any and of every kind had been courteously but firmly and resolutely rejected.

His rejection of honours was based on two points:

(*a*) A horror of arousing any more jealousy than already existed in the Emperor's official and unofficial *entourage*; and a desire that he—Marmaduke—should not be brought into greater contact or have more official relations with this *entourage* than was absolutely necessary.

It is needless to say that, like all reformers—especially reformers who had attained any degree of success—he had hosts of enemies. Consequently he knew that every movement on his part required to be taken with the utmost circumspection. The slightest false step would probably mean ignominy for himself and disaster for his cause.

(*b*) He declared that his desire for the welfare of mankind in general, and the German nation in particular, far outweighed personal ambition.

Marmaduke's position, therefore, was no different from that which he had hitherto occupied, namely, that of a private person who had the honour and the opportunity of offering suggestions to the Emperor. Let others lead, let others command, let others hold official posts, let others receive honours, Marmaduke was quite satisfied if he could merely influence.

He never took undue advantage of the peculiar position in which he found himself. He was always bold, always outspoken, but scrupulously courteous to his august patron. The Emperor might be familiar—he was always partial to Arthur's pseudonym, and generally made use of the diminutive "Duke" as a Christian name—but Marmaduke never presumed upon this familiarity.

Such, very roughly and in outline, were the relative positions of these two striking characters, the dreamer and the monarch; two characters who were destined to impress their personality in such a striking manner upon the world's history.

Fortunately Providence withholds from us a foresight of the future. If these two men could have foreseen the tragedy in which, before many years, they were both destined to take such a prominent part, in all probability one of them would have shrunk back in dismay from the task before him.

CHAPTER XVI.

SHOWING HOW THE COURSE OF DIPLOMACY, LIKE TRUE LOVE, DOES NOT ALWAYS RUN SMOOTHLY.

MANY months had elapsed since the general election. The German ship had been exposed to a constant succession of gusts, squalls, and storms.

The political sea was still very agitated. The good ship had hitherto successfully encountered all this dirty weather, but the anxiety of her captain and crew had not abated. A feeling prevailed that some time would elapse before they would again float in smooth waters.

The Bill for Amending the Government and Constitution of Alsace-Lorraine had, despite the opposition, duly passed through all its stages. A vote of the two provinces had followed, and, as every one anticipated, the result was overwhelmingly in favour of their recession to France.

Alsace-Lorraine was jubilant and France was grateful. The spirit of revenge had evidently disappeared from the minds of Frenchmen. But had the policy of restitution, of peace, and of goodwill produced those favourable results which had been foretold by Marmaduke? We shall see.

Let us enter a room in the Imperial Palace in Berlin. It is a capacious apartment. There are magnificent curtains to windows and doors. The carpet is a dream of sombre splendour and soft comfort. The furniture is of old oak, massive and beautifully carved. The numerous chairs and lounges are of ample dimensions and upholstered in the most choice leather. But the room is evidently a business library. For there are several telephones and other telegraphic receivers and transmitters, also some typewriting machines. In the place of the books one usually sees round the walls of a library, are elaborately bound and lettered folios of official documents. On one side is a massive and handsome escritoire fitted with pigeon holes and nests of drawers. In fact, the apartment and its appointments form such a combination of luxury, elegance, and business as is fit for the use of an emperor. It is called the "Telephone Room."

Seated before the escritoire is Marmaduke busily engaged in perusing several voluminous documents. He looks serious. He takes up one after another and scans them; the serious look deepens. At last he comes to one which is rather more bulky than the rest. It absorbs his attention. He leans back in his chair, reads it carefully, then re-reads it. The serious look melts into one of anxiety. The lines deepen on his brow. His habitually pale face becomes a shade paler. Let us glance at this document. It is a private and confidential dispatch addressed to the Imperial Chancellor, Count Von Werner, from Prince Sax, Imperial Ambassador at Paris.

The following are a few extracts :—

* * * * * *

"I have carefully carried out the instructions contained in your Excellency's despatch of the

3rd inst., but I exceedingly regret to be compelled to report that at present I see no probability of a complete and successful issue to the line of policy laid down by the Imperial Government."

* * * * * *

"Let me recapitulate the situation. Your Excellency will remember that the Bill for Amending the Government and Constitution of Alsace-Lorraine was introduced with the object of finding an amicable solution to the terrible military problem which confronted Europe. The recession of the two provinces was intended to conciliate France to such an extent as to render a Germano-French alliance possible. This alliance once an established fact, all danger of an immediate war would disappear. A general treaty of peace would then be possible, and Europe would be within measurable distance of a partial disarmament. Such a sequence of conditions would naturally conduce to the prosperity of all countries affected.

"The first portion of this bold and novel policy was carried out. The Bill became law. The conquered provinces voted for their re-union to France. The French Government was gratified, Alsace-Lorraine no longer belonged to Germany.

* * * * * *

"A change had certainly come over the attitude of France to Germany. The Frenchman may be said, in his thoughts and sentiments, to have fraternised with the German.

"The time for taking further action had, therefore, apparently arrived.

"Our first business, as indicated by your Excellency, was to loosen that chain which has hitherto bound France and Russia so firmly together—in fact, to detach France from the double alliance. It was felt that until this bond could be relaxed, any action we might take for the establishment of closer relations with the French Government would be futile. But further progress, however, on those desirable lines which I have indicated, seems to be at present impossible. The French ministers have hitherto firmly resisted all overtures on my part for holding a conference of the nature suggested by your Excellency.

* * * * * *

"I need scarcely say that the resources of diplomacy have been exhausted in attempting to bring about a re-arrangement on an amicable basis of the existing relations between the German and French Governments, but unfortunately without success. I have had numerous interviews with the President of the French Republic, and with most of the French Ministers, especially with Monsieur Emile Augustin, the French Premier; and while they are all exceedingly cordial in their communications, none of them hold out the slightest hope that the French Government will be able, at present, to take into serious consideration any modification of existing treaties, or the preparation of new ones in the direction desired by the Imperial Government.

"Monsieur Augustin prefers to state this in unequivocal language, rather than enter into pourparlers which will merely have the effect of shelving the question, and he considers that his frankness, in all the circumstances, will be fully appreciated.

* * * * * *

"I have reason to believe that arguments almost amounting to an ultimatum, have been addressed by the Russian Government to the French Ministry, and with success, in order to maintain the existing Franco-Russian alliance in its integrity."

* * * * * *

While Marmaduke was reading this dispatch, a curtain in front of one of the doors was seen to move, and the Emperor noiselessly entered the apartment and seated himself near the escritoire. Marmaduke was so much engrossed with the document he was perusing, that he was perfectly oblivious to the presence of his august visitor.

Presently Marmaduke laid down the paper with a sigh, saw the Emperor, started, and rose from his seat.

"I am afraid I startled you, Duke. Pray be seated. Well, what do you think of the situation now? I see you have been closely occupied with the dispatch of Prince Sax. Have you read the other dispatches and reports? There is the same tale from the French Ambassador here; the same tale everywhere. Diplomacy is evidently at a deadlock. The

French are grateful, cordial, friendly, but they are not to be moved from the double alliance.

"England is as cold in the matter as usual. She throws out the usual plea of neutrality.

"With Italy bankrupt, Austria reticent, France polite, England neutral, Russia hostile; Germany does not seem to obtain much assistance from other governments in promoting the new *régime*. You prophesied a sequence of events, Duke. They don't seem to follow one another so smoothly as you imagined. If you remember, we were to have a grateful France; existing treaties were to vanish into thin air; a German-French alliance was to spring into existence; and glorious results were to follow. There are already ominous mutterings and grumblings in Germany at the non-fulfilment of our sanguine prognostications. The press and the people are openly saying we have sacrificed Alsace-Lorraine for nothing. I must, I will alter the situation! What am I to do now?"

"The situation is certainly grave," replied Marmaduke; "but in the first place I think your Majesty must allow events a little more time to develop naturally; and in the second place diplomacy is working on the wrong lines.

"We have witnessed the re-birth of Christianity in Europe, sire, but this re-born Christianity has not yet attained vigorous growth. It must have time for development before it can exert its proper strength.

"Your Majesty has undertaken to move Europe— a ponderous mass. It cannot move fast at first; it must acquire momentum. And to do this takes time. Follow the same line of argument with France. In the course of years France has acquired a momentum in a certain direction. Can your Majesty imagine that the movement of the whole mass can be stopped and sent in the opposite direction without a considerable expenditure of time as well as energy?

"Again, the usual diplomatic procedure may have suited the old *régime*, but it certainly will not suit the new.

"What have the German diplomats been doing? Actually trying to pulverise the Franco-Russian alliance. In other words, as a preliminary to a universal peace, they have actually been waging a diplomatic war against Russia! Can you wonder that diplomacy has failed?"

"What would you do then?" said the Emperor; "abolish diplomacy?"

"Certainly not; but diplomacy must be untaught a great many lessons it has been learning for centuries. In plain words, your Majesty, is not diplomacy, stripped of its politeness, its plausibility, its—shall I say—hypocrisy, merely a synonym for trickery, plotting, counter-plotting, taking selfish advantage, fair or unfair, of other Governments; cheating opponents anywhere and anyhow? Will these command success in the new order of things which has been so happily introduced by your Majesty and the German Government? It will doubtless take a long time for diplomacy to alter motives and change the direction of its energies, but this will have to be done, or diplomats and emperors will be called upon to pay a severe penalty."

"Say on, Duke. Tell me what you suggest; but remember, there is nothing so fatal as failure, and any man's advice is only valuable just so long as it points the way to success. Neither the German Emperor nor Germany can afford to fail! Rather than risk this we had better revert to militarism and put our trust in Queljanite."

"Diplomacy has failed, sire; let diplomacy bear the blame. There is a deadlock, and, so far as the respective Governments are concerned, the double alliance is as firmly established as ever. Is it not so, your Majesty?"

"Exactly," ejaculated the Kaiser.

"But whatever a certain set of men who call themselves the French ministry may say, can your Majesty doubt for a single instant that the people of France and the people of Germany are ready and anxious to form a friendly and peaceful alliance?"

"Very likely; but how will this fact solve the problem?" interrupted the Emperor.

Marmaduke took no notice of the interruption, but continued: "Also, is there a single doubt that these two peoples would be only too glad if Russia joined them in the same peaceful alliance? It is true that the Franco-Russian alliance has been, to a certain extent, responsible for the terrible military problem, and it may be equally true that whilst this alliance exists in its present state, the peace of Europe is menaced. But is it fair, is it just, is it in harmony with the new order of conciliation and righteousness, that German diplomats should treat Russia with implied hatred, malice, and all uncharitableness? What is required now is another bold stroke."

"What is that bold stroke to be?" said the Kaiser.

"Nothing less, your Majesty, than the capture of the French people as you captured the German."

"How, Duke? With another manifesto?"

"Yes, sire, but a manifesto of a different character. Ministries and diplomats must be pushed on one side, and the knot which cannot be untied must be cut."

For many hours, far into the night, with few and slight intervals for refreshments, the Emperor and Marmaduke were engaged in earnest conversation. They littered the Telephone Room with notes and memoranda, and frequently made use of one or other of the telephones. When, at length, their labours for that night were concluded, the project, whatever it was, had been carefully and exhaustively thought out.

CHAPTER XVII.

AN ACCOUNT OF A MISSION UNDERTAKEN BY MARMADUKE, AND THE RECEPTION WHICH HE MET WITH.

A VERY simple announcement which appeared in *The Times*, and was at once telegraphed to Berlin, Paris, and other centres, excited a good deal of comment in official as well as unofficial circles, both in France and Germany. The announcement was as follows :

"We have excellent authority for stating that Marmaduke will shortly undertake a mission to France. The precise nature and object of this mission are not disclosed, but it is believed to be of a semi-social, semi-political character. It will be entirely unofficial, and will probably be found to have some bearing upon recent political events, to which it will doubtless form a sequel."

On the one hand official politicians wondered what would be next sprung upon them. They were inclined to resent any movement which did not emanate from an official source, or of which officialism had no cognizance.

On the other hand, the general public were curious as to the exact identity of the still strange and mysterious Marmaduke, and rejoiced that the opportunity would shortly be afforded them of gratifying this curiosity.

Politicians and public were not long kept in suspense.

Within a fortnight of the date of the announcement in *The Times*, it was rumoured that Marmaduke would commence his mission.

The exact time of his departure from Berlin was not known many hours beforehand. But the notice was sufficiently long for numbers of Berliners to gather in the streets, and quite a crowd to assemble at the Lehrter railway station, from which he was to take his departure. He drove quietly and alone, without any escort whatever. Very little cheering was heard in the streets. Many people, however, bowed their recognition, and a number of handkerchiefs were waved from windows.

Although no actual hostility was shown, his reception was certainly not enthusiastic. This apathy was probably due to a combination of causes. Those who were inclined to be friendly, were doubtless too much animated by curiosity to be demonstrative. For it must be remembered that this was the first time that Marmaduke had appeared publicly in the streets of Berlin. Those who were certainly hostile to Marmaduke and all his ways were apathetic, for they had lost the sting of their hostility in the belief that the bolt which had been shot against militarism had fallen short of its mark and had dropped harmlessly to the ground. In other words, they thought that the Emperor and Marmaduke were powerless to solve the military problem in a peaceful manner.

Added to this, mutterings were increasing in number and volume to the effect that Germany had made sacrifices in vain, and that a permanent peace was as far off as ever.

We do not intend to give a detailed report of Marmaduke's tour and progress. Sufficient to say that upon quitting Berlin he went straight to the north-eastern frontier of France; visited all the principal towns in eastern and central France; made his way to the south as far as Marseilles and Toulon, then to the south-west, taking in Bayonne, then Bordeaux; then further west as far as Brest; thence worked his way to the north as far as Calais, and finally retraced his steps to Amiens, the last town before he visited Paris.

At Mézierès, the first town on French soil at which he stopped, he would have been glad to go straight to the hotel. He was worn out, more with mental anxiety than with travelling. But a large crowd received him at the station and were clamorous for a speech. In response he stood up in the carriage and said:

"Friends, I am glad to be able to tell you that the message I have is a message of peace. The object I desire is an amicable *rapprochement* of the French and German peoples. I desire to see the two nations in friendly agreement in wishes, aims, and objects. I shall be perfectly frank and open in what I say to the French people. There is no ulterior motive. The German holds out his hand; will the Frenchman grasp that hand? I want that grasp to bind the hearts of the two peoples in a bond of brotherhood. In order to accomplish this end I have undertaken a mission. This mission is simply and solely to advocate that a conference shall be held consisting of representatives of both nations, the object of which conference will be to formulate a mutually satisfactory agreement of peace, which shall be of a permanent character."

Whether the French ministers looked upon Marmaduke and his mission with favour, or the reverse, at any rate the local authorities received private instructions not to hinder his mission ; and the French people were determined to hear what he had to say. Everyone was anxious to see the man who had been instrumental in the restoration of the two provinces to France.

Many prominent men in the towns which he proposed to visit constituted themselves his advance agents, hired buildings in which he could speak, and organised public meetings. At some places receptions were arranged ; and at more than one town he received an invitation to a municipal or other ball. He did not object to attend a ball or a reception ; on the contrary, he seemed to have lost all his reticence, all his reserve. He was willing to meet the people anywhere, everywhere—in the ballroom, the *salon*, the street, or at the hotel which happened to be his headquarters for the time. But he gave his decided preference to the platform with the crowded audience before him, the more crowded the better.

It will be impossible to reproduce a tithe of the speeches he made or the arguments he used. We can only give a few extracts, and these extracts will give but a very poor idea of his speeches. For the electric sympathy of his spoken words can never be translated into printer's ink or printer's type. In one speech he said:

"You ask me if my aim is political. It is. But my object is not merely to substitute one alliance for another. You have had for many years two alliances opposed to one another: the double alliance and the triple alliance. Each member of these two alliances has emphatically announced that his object is a peaceful one. Granted. But does the present situation conduce to peace? Look at Europe as one vast camp. Look how the enormous opposing forces have armed themselves. Look how each of the countries involved has drained and is draining itself of its treasure, its manhood, its intellect, its resources, its life. For what? To preserve peace? The idea savours of insanity. No. The only possible result of these enormous armaments, these enormous sacrifices, will be war; and war sooner rather than later.

"If, then, these opposing alliances are making for war—which, it is alleged, not one of the signatories desires—cannot the problem be solved by substituting for these two alliances a single peaceful alliance; an alliance of all powers and interests immediately concerned—France, Germany, Russia, Austria, Italy, as well as of those other countries indirectly concerned? Is a European Bund, an alliance of peace, impossible? No! Then let us point the way by bringing into existence a friendly understanding between the two chief factors in this terrible European military problem, France and Germany.

"No one denies that whilst one country is willing to forget the victories of the first Napoleon, the other country is willing to forget the defeats of the third Napoleon.

"You may say that the fact of Germany possessing such a deadly and menacing engine of war and destruction as Queljanite, forms an insuperable bar to an amicable agreement. Not at all. I think you need not apprehend the slightest difficulty in connection with Queljanite. For should a Conference be held and a satisfactory conclusion arrived at, obviously the control or suppression of this, as well as of any other deadly weapon of war, must be at the disposal of the associated Governments.

"Germany wants nothing but what is honourable, just, right, equitable. France desires exactly the same. It is impossible that a number of representatives of each country, sitting round one table, cannot devise an arrangement which shall be perfectly satisfactory to both countries. Once the conference has arrived at such an arrangement, Europe will be within measurable distance of a disarmament or partial disarmament. This carried out gradually and judiciously, under conditions carefully elaborated, will do more than anything else to restore happiness, contentment, and prosperity to those European nations which are now groaning under burdens too grievous to be borne."

The French deputies at first kept aloof, but afterwards were gradually attracted, until by the time the tour was nearly completed, Marmaduke had a large following of deputies who were almost as enthusiastic in advocating a peace conference as he was.

The French Anarchical Socialists, not a very large, but a very noisy and troublesome party, were opposed to Marmaduke. They denounced what they called his "milk and water" proposals. They doubtless preferred, for their own purposes, that France should seethe with discontent, rather than be quiet and prosperous.

Other Socialists, those who aimed at social reforms under a Republican Government, the Guèsde, and that rapidly-increasing organisation which was the outcome of the municipal Socialism formulated at the St. Etienne Congress of 1882 by M. Brousse, warmly welcomed Marmaduke and gave him all the assistance in their power.

In addressing a crowded meeting in the Cirque d' Hiver, at Bordeaux, he was statistical. He said :

"It is true, thank God, that the war tension is not quite so great as it was a short time ago. But, even with the immediate danger of war removed, have you realised what the present military conditions mean for France? They mean that the standing army at the present moment numbers 794,000 men; that France has 89 ironclads and monitors, 478 frigates, ships, and steamers, manned by over 100,000 officers and men ; that at the sound of the trumpet France could place in the field 28 Army Corps, and to maintain them the nation would have to pay 23,425,000 francs a day,* or nearly 170,000,000 a week ; that these figures represent roughly an increase of 50 per cent. on the figures of 1890.

"Think of what the military situation means to the opposed alliances. France and Russia can now put into the field 8,156,956 men, 14,880 field guns, and 2,213,000 horses. While Germany, Austria, and

* £937,000 a day.

Italy can muster 8,911,914 men, 12,276 field guns, and 1,221,000 horses.

"Such an armed peace is almost as disastrous for you as war. Conscription is crushing you. The taxation to enable such a state of things to be maintained, is draining you of your life's blood. The military burdens are at the foundation of the terrible agricultural distress and the present overwhelming industrial crisis.

"The military problem has completely eclipsed the social problem. Burdens are heaped upon burdens, until hope becomes a mockery and life a waking nightmare. Would you throw off these burdens? Would you make life for your sons and daughters worth living? Then, with an overwhelming, irresistible voice ask your Government to consent to a friendly conference with Germany. Ask your Government to invite your other European neighbours to join the conference."

With exquisite delicacy and tact, he never once alluded to the restoration of the two provinces, nor did he hint directly or indirectly that France had received any benefit or was under any obligation to Germany.

Marmaduke did not employ the arts of oratory. He spoke, simply, calmly, quietly, but what he said carried more weight than fervid declamation. Yet cool and calm as he was, his enthusiasm was at white heat.

He was a man with the tender heart of a woman, yet virile to the finger tips.

As prophet, as religious enthusiast, as social reformer, as politician of the new order—the order which took "righteousness" for its watchword, and the golden rule for its code of morals—he possessed a combination of qualities which were irresistible. But besides these qualities, he possessed the power invaluable to any public speaker, of touching a sympathetic chord in the hearts of his hearers, and of keeping that chord vibrating.

It may be objected that he repeated and reiterated his arguments. Granted. But as the prophet of old went up and down preaching the gospel of punishment and destruction, repeating and reiterating, "Yet forty days and Nineveh shall be overthrown"; so Marmaduke went up and down France, preaching the gospel of good will, reiterating and ringing the changes on love, peace, friendship, brotherhood, until curiosity grew into admiration, and admiration into enthusiasm.

For years afterwards, the people in the provinces of France were haunted by the memory of that pale clean-shaven face, those piercing sunken eyes, that look of terrible earnestness, that absorbing manner, that intense yet calm exterior, that thrilling personality, which they were destined never to look on again.

At last Marmaduke's mission was ended. It now only remained for him to visit Paris. He longed, yet dreaded to enter the capital, ascertain the decision of the French ministers on the matter, and discover whether his mission had succeeded or failed.

CHAPTER XVIII.

MARMADUKE VISITS PARIS, MEETS WITH AN ENTHUSIASTIC RECEPTION, AND RETURNS TO BERLIN EXHAUSTED, BUT SUCCESSFUL.

PARIS has been called the microcosm of France. In fact, it has been said that Paris *is* France, in miniature, concentrated, and focussed. Whether there is a modicum of truth in this statement or not, Marmaduke felt that, unless he could capture Paris, he would have to write down his mission a failure.

Consequently, he concluded that upon visiting Paris, he would have to put forth a mighty final effort. He would have to marshal all his arguments, and concentrate, in a few speeches in the capital, the matter contained in a vast number of his speeches in the provinces.

He was still as enthusiastic and energetic as ever, but he knew that he could not bear the strain much longer. Excitement and mental anxiety were beginning to tell upon him. He therefore braced up his nerves for the final effort, but dreaded the ordeal.

The unexpected happened, however. Just when he thought that his heaviest task still lay before him, he suddenly discovered that his work was finished and his mission ended. Before he had time to strike a blow, Paris capitulated, and his first drive through the streets of the capital turned out to be simply a triumphal entry. Had he been a French general returning from the subjugation of a hostile continent, he could not have been received with more tokens of popular enthusiasm.

When once the sympathy of the French people is gained, they are generous to a fault ; and they show no inclination to put such limits to their generosity as the more phlegmatic Teutons or Anglo-Saxons. The French temperament is essentially mercurial, and no nation in Europe can exhibit more indications of the intoxication of wild delight, when once thoroughly aroused, than the French. In no capital in the world can more excitement be imparted to the progress of a popular favourite through the streets than in Paris.

When Marmaduke alighted from the train at the terminus of the Northern Railway, he was received with cordiality by the Prefect of the Seine, a number of deputies, and representatives of the Paris muncipality, Socialist societies, and other bodies and organisations. Some of them presented him with addresses of welcome, congratulation, and support. The platform was decorated with the taste and delicacy characteristic of the Frenchman. There was no crowd in the station, but the space on the platform for the length of the train, and in the *salle d'attente*, where luggage is usually examined, were fairly well occupied by privileged spectators, a broad carpeted gangway being reserved from the railway carriage to the exit doors of the station.

The ceremony inside the station was soon over. The presentation of addresses and a few words spoken on both sides, did not occupy many minutes. Marmaduke was then conducted along the platform through the *salle d'attente* to his carriage at the outer doors.

Then he saw a sight which he never forgot. The streets were artistically decorated, flags fluttered, various inscriptions of welcome were visible. The monumental façade of the magnificent new Gare du Nord (which had not been erected many years, and was one of the finest railway stations in Europe) as well as the buildings which surrounded it, had put on holiday attire. The sun shone brilliantly, the sky was of that deep, clear blue so frequently associated with Italian scenery. But it was not the decorations, the architecture, the blue sky, or the magnificent sunshine which riveted Marmaduke's attention. It was the sea of faces which he saw on either side.

There were faces everywhere; the whole space in front of him as well as in the adjacent streets was packed with people. There were faces at all the windows, and every balcony or projection which could safely hold a human being, held one. Faces looked up at him from the ground, and looked down upon him from the roofs.

The moment he stepped into his carriage and the people saw him, handkerchiefs fluttered, hats waved, and a mighty roar burst forth. It was more like thunder than cheers.

The sight of a vast mass of men and women has a strange effect upon the most phlegmatic individual. It can therefore be imagined how Marmaduke was thrilled through and through as he stood up, gazed at the sight before him, heard the continuous roar, and knew that these vast numbers were paying popular homage, not so much to the man, as the cause which he championed.

For a short time the carriage could not stir, so closely were the people wedged together. At last a slight progress was made, and the carriage began to move. The pace was so slow that the crowd had ample opportunity to gaze on the features of the popular hero. The carriage progressed at a walking pace across the Rue de la Fayette and into the Boulevard de Strasbourg. It passed down this fine avenue, and then traversed those historic streets so dear to the hearts of visitors as well as Parisians, the Boulevards St. Denis, Bonne Nouvelle, Poissonière, Montmartre, des Italiens, des Capucines, until it drew up at its present destination, the Grand Hotel. From start to finish the scene and the sounds were the same. There was not a single break in the continuity of the sea of faces, the fluttering of handkerchiefs, the waving of hats, the swelling and surging masses, or the prolonged roar of applause.

Delighted, cheered, astonished, bewildered, Marmaduke sank into an easy chair in a private sitting-room in the Grand Hotel, thoroughly exhausted with his magnificent welcome.

For several days he was compelled to be quiet; nervous exhaustion had prostrated him. He therefore kept his room and was invisible to visitors. It is needless to say that hundreds of callers of all grades of society left cards and messages at the hotel. Congratulatory telegrams and letters fluttered down upon the exhausted Marmaduke in hundreds from all parts and from all parties.

In a fortnight, however, he was sufficiently recovered to receive visitors.

The first person to whom he was visible was Prince Sax, the German Ambassador at Paris.

From the moment that Marmaduke saw the reception which awaited him, he instinctively felt that the success of his mission was assured. But he was scarcely prepared for the news brought to him by the Prince. The French Ministry had not only agreed to send accredited representatives to a conference having for its object the preparation of a treaty of peace upon a permanent basis, but a triangular correspondence had taken place between the respective Governments of Germany, France, and Russia, and each and all had at once come to a similar agreement. This news, particularly as regards Russia, astonished Marmaduke, for he knew that Russia had hitherto been the chief agent in opposing the proposed conference; consequently he could not quite understand Russia's sudden acquiescence. But the Russian was astute, more astute than Marmaduke imagined—as he subsequently discovered.

It was further mutually agreed between the three Powers mentioned, that the conference should be held in the capital of a first-class Power, a neutral one, and one that so far as the double and triple alliances were concerned, was disinterested. England fulfilled all these conditions, and it was generally understood that in London the conference would be held. Dispatches had already been sent to Austria and Italy, detailing what had been decided by the three Powers, subject to the acquiescence of the other members of the two alliances. And that acquiescence had been given by these two Powers.

As Prince Sax naïvely remarked to Marmaduke—

"Of course Austria and Italy have consented to the proposals. They cannot afford to keep their fingers out of any European pie cooked by Germany, France, and Russia."

It is needless for us to give a detailed account of Marmaduke's public movements during the three or four weeks which elapsed between his entry into Paris and his return to Berlin. He received and returned numbers of visits from distinguished as well as humble men. The President of the Republic honoured him with a call, and had a long and interesting conversation with him, and he was received at the Elysée with the courtesy and etiquette due to a visitor of much more distinguished rank than a plain English commoner.

One of the very few functions in which he allowed himself to take part, was the reception by the Municipality at the Hotel de Ville. Those who are aware of the enormous number of visitors capable of being received in this historic structure, and those who know the democratic character of the Paris Municipality, can readily appreciate the scene on that memorable night when Marmaduke passed through throng after throng and crowd after crowd of enthusiastic admirers.

He was still suffering from the reaction, and his nervous system was in a very weak condition when he quitted Paris. At his urgent request, and in consideration of his state of health, he was allowed to leave the city of his triumphs privately and practically *incognito*.

He left the Gare du Nord at a little after eight o'clock in the morning. Prince Sax and two or three friends were the only persons who accompanied him to the station and wished him *bon voyage*. He felt he sadly needed rest, and was thankful that his duty did not compel him to be the cynosure of thousands of eyes. He fondly hoped that he would reach Berlin unnoticed and unrecognised. He passed through Erquelinnes about midday, Liege about three o'clock, reached the German frontier about five o'clock, and was due at Cologne about 7.45 p.m.

But before he had reached the famous cathedral city the secret had leaked out. Somehow it was known that Marmaduke was in the train, and during the hour and a half's delay at Cologne, which the service of trains necessitated, there was a considerable movement amongst the people to catch a sight of the popular hero.

Meantime the news had been flashed to Berlin, and it was soon known in the capital that the 9.30 p.m. sleeping car express from Cologne, due at Berlin at 7.30 a.m. the next morning, would convey Marmaduke.

The Berliners determined that they would atone for the apathy which they had shown at his departure. This change in their attitude was, no doubt, partially due to the mere fact of his success. But besides this, the conscience of the good Berliners was evidently pricked that they had allowed him to quit them so quietly; so they determined to make amends.

Although it was so early in the morning, vast crowds had assembled in the streets and at the

Lehrter Railway Station a considerable time before the train was due.

There were necessarily very few decorations, but the enormous numbers of people made ample compensation for the paucity of flags, etc. The reception was truly a grand one, as well for Marmaduke as for the cause of righteousness, peace, and good-will to men.

The following are extracts from a telegram which appeared in the *Daily News* the next morning, from its Berlin Correspondent:

"Punctually at 7.30 a.m. the train steamed into the station. A minute of commotion and suspense, and then Marmaduke left the carriage. His face was deadly pale, his eyes were lustreless, and his usually upright form was slightly bent. He was evidently ill.

"When he left the carriage, the Crown Prince stepped forward and officially reported that he had been ordered to welcome Marmaduke on behalf of His Majesty, and to further state that the Emperor had placed some of the rooms in the Imperial Castle at his—Marmaduke's—disposal. They then shook hands heartily, and after Marmaduke had spoken to the other gentlemen present, they left the station arm in arm.

"Now began a triumphal ride in an open state carriage, drawn by four horses, with postillions and escorted in front and in rear by half a squadron of cuirassiers; past the officers of the general staff; past the old Column of Victory on the Königs Platz, the memorial of a blood and iron *régime*; past the newer Imperial Houses of

Parliament, where a departure from that *régime* was inaugurated; through the Brandenburg Gate, and along the historical Avenue Unter den Linden. The crowds were quite as vast as those which greeted him upon his memorable entry into Paris. Shouts of 'hoch, hoch!' broke from the crowds; handkerchiefs were waved by the ladies and hats by the men. But the applause was hushed as the carriage slowly made its way through the crowds.

"The extreme pallor of Marmaduke was so striking, and the effort to maintain his composure was so apparent and painful, that there was an instinctive inclination to greet him with respectful silence, rather than noise.

* * * * * *

"Marmaduke sat on the left of the Crown Prince, who leaned back, etiquette forbidding him in the presence of his visitor to respond to the greetings of the people. Upon alighting at the palace, the Emperor appeared, surrounded by the members of his suite and many others, and welcomed Marmaduke most heartily. The latter was deeply moved, and could scarcely master his emotion. Later on, the Empress appeared, to welcome the distinguished guest. At the subsequent breakfast, only the Emperor, the Empress, and Marmaduke were present.

* * * * * *

"In the course of the morning all the ministers, and many of the ambassadors and other distinguished people, left their cards for Marmaduke; and the Imperial Chancellor, Count von

Werner, also called, and had a long conversation with the Emperor's guest."

Thus returned Marmaduke to Berlin. His ride through the streets of the German capital was certainly different from that other ride through the streets of the French capital. But he could fully appreciate, as perhaps no one else could, the kindness and consideration, as well as the warmth of welcome, displayed by all classes of Berlin society from the Emperor downwards.

His entry into Paris was a historical triumph. His entry into Berlin was an affectionate welcome home.

CHAPTER XIX

MARMADUKE RECRUITS HIS HEALTH AT FELIXSTOWE, BUT FINALLY HEARS NEWS, WHICH GREATLY AGITATES HIM AND ACCELERATES HIS DEPARTURE.

THE reader must now accompany us to Felixstowe, the well known East Anglian wateringplace, where Marmaduke is staying for the benefit of his health.

After his return to Berlin, he still continued to look and feel very unwell. His medical adviser, as well as his numerous friends, recommended perfect rest for a time. Ostensibly he followed this advice, and returned to London, but was so injudicious as immediately to commence working hard upon a series of draft proposals and suggested clauses, as well as arguments and data supporting them, which he intended to submit to the approaching great Peace Conference in London. For it goes without saying that he had received an invitation to attend this conference.

He had just concluded this work and felt that he could now take a short, well-earned rest, when, the tension on his system being removed, the reaction came and a serious collapse occurred. This time his weakness did not yield to the usual remedies, and a complete cessation from work for some considerable time became necessary. So great was his nerve prostration that he ceased to feel interest in anything—a bad sign. He knew, without being told by the physicians, that his ultimate restoration to health depended upon absolute rest for his brain for some time to come. He was told that he had no organic disease, only functional derangement, but one of the doctors naïvely said: " The best prescription I can give you is to go to a quiet, bracing place, amuse yourself, lounge about, put your hands in your pockets, and think of nothing."

His presence at meetings of the conference, for some time to come, was now out of the question, although the members would have the benefit of the notes and memoranda he had already prepared.

The air of Felixstowe was bracing, and he had several years previously derived great benefit from it. The place was sufficiently large to be cheerful; was not too noisy on the one hand, and not too quiet on the other. Therefore, he chose Felixstowe; and arrangements were made that his visit should be strictly private, so that he could lead a lazy life there, unnoticed and unknown.

His friends naturally desired that he should be accompanied, otherwise they feared he would be a prey to depression. But, intensely sympathetic and companionable as he always was, just now he preferred to be quite alone. Loneliness for him did not necessarily imply depression of spirits.

As a compromise, it was arranged that his old friend, Colonel Wolff, who had at first so persistently opposed his schemes, and who was still attached to the London embassy, should accompany him to

Felixstowe, remain with him a short time, and subsequently visit him at intervals.

Although Felixstowe was his temporary home, and he had contemplated attending the conference in London, yet he regarded Berlin as his headquarters, and it was here that he kept all his private papers.

His sojourn at Felixstowe was uneventful. He amused himself by sauntering about the place and noting the many changes and the rapid growth which had taken place since he had last visited it.

Houses, fronted by a broad esplanade, now stretched uninterruptedly from the Bath Hotel to the boundary of Landguard Fort. Villas were also dotted along what were once golf links on the cliffs, from Felixstowe right to the mouth of the Deben, where quite an aristocratic watering-place had sprung up on the site of old Bawdsey.

The Ordnance Hotel, which he had known so well, existed no more. Exactly opposite the site which it once occupied was the new railway station. This superseded the original station, which conflicting landed interests had succeeded in placing in such an inconvenient position.

A broad boulevard called Pier Avenue, lined with trees on each side, reached from the new railway station to the beach. The Martello Tower near this spot had been demolished, and of the ground which it once occupied a very picturesque public garden had been formed, with zig-zag paths cut in the hill-side.

There was another new feature which greatly interested Marmaduke. Opposite the end of the handsome avenue leading from the station, consequently in the centre of Felixstowe Bay and equidistant from each end of the handsome esplanade, was a fine pier over half-a-mile long. This was one of the most attractive features of the place, and was the feature to which Felixstowe mainly owed its rapid growth and present importance.

In a modest house to the right of the avenue and facing the sea, a house which still retained its original —but now obsolete—name of "Martello House," lodged Marmaduke.

After a short time, when his recuperative powers succeeded in asserting themselves, he began to enjoy himself in his own way.

He loved to pace the broad Esplanade or walk along the beach close to the sea; watch the rhythmic roll of the waves as they came in straight from the North Sea; hear the merry voices and see the delighted faces of the children as they played on the beach. When he was disinclined to walk, he would sit in the verandah of his temporary home, drink in health with the ozone, and abandon himself to that delicious intoxication of inactivity which is sometimes so beneficial to the worn brain.

He loved to wander up and down the various steep ascents which led from the beach to the interior of the town, and gaze on the really splendid panorama, which was visible from the top of the cliff, of Harwich Harbour, busy Parkeston Quay, and the coast-line from Walton landmark almost to Bawdsey Ferry.

He loved to walk up the long pier, take a seat in one of the convenient glazed shelters at the end, and watch through a powerful binocular the Continental boats pass to and fro as they entered or quitted the harbour, or the movements of the men on board the Cork lightship.

When he was tired of his binocular, he would turn his attention to the small children who were assiduously engaged in fishing from the pier-head for flat fish, which they wanted, but seldom caught; and pulling up small green crabs, which they invariably caught, but never wanted—a system of compensation which the small folk in question by no means appreciated.

When tired of watching sea or children he would enter the pavilion on the pier, and either listen to a concert or watch whatever other entertainment happened to be the programme for the day.

He loved to lounge in the vicinity of the railway station, lazily watch the trains arrive and depart, and as lazily watch the passengers and luggage come and go. Without perhaps always following his physician's instructions, to "put his hands in his pockets," he nevertheless did his level best to carry out the remaining portion of the injunction and "think of nothing."

One day he was watching the arrival of a train, when his attention was arrested by seeing a gentleman alight, who was carrying a portmanteau, upon which the initials A. H. M. were conspicuously painted. This was a coincidence, not a very striking one, but still a coincidence, for Marmaduke had caused the same initials, A. H. M. (meaning Arthur Hardy Marmaduke) to be painted on his portmanteau. Moreover, Marmaduke's portmanteau was the only article which bore these identical initials, his linen being marked A. H.

The strange gentleman, whoever he was, carried his portmanteau to the Bath Hotel omnibus, entered it, and Marmaduke saw him no more.

There the matter ended, so far as Marmaduke himself was concerned ; for, although the incident doubtless gave rise to a passing thought in his mind, he had not sufficient curiosity to call at the Bath Hotel and ascertain the identity of A. H. M., nor had he a wish to attract attention to himself by making any inquiries.

There was no mystery, however, for on the following Saturday *The East Anglian Daily Times*, in its local edition, included the name of Mr. A. H. Morrison, Harlesden, London, in the list of visitors staying at the Bath Hotel.

So the time sped on at Felixstowe, and Marmaduke gradually regained his strength. The progress had been so slow that he was scarcely conscious of it. The first indication he had of a return of health was a desire, at first slight, then becoming more intense, to take an active part in the great conference which had already sat a considerable number of times.

Marmaduke at last began to fret and chafe at his enforced idleness, and his medical advisers considered it would not be detrimental to his health, but rather the reverse, that he should receive reports from the conference. Accordingly a *precis* of some of the most important of the proceedings was sent him from time to time.

He then learnt that the Prime Minister, the Duke of Dalmeny, had been appointed chairman, partly because etiquette demanded that the chief representative of the Power in whose country the conference was held should preside, and partly because England was neutral and disinterested.

He learnt that the report containing his suggestions and draft clauses had been very well received.

He learnt that several of the preliminary clauses had been settled, but that further progress was so slow, that a deadlock was feared.

He learnt, as much from inference as from actual statement, that Russia presented every possible obstacle, was moving heaven and earth to render the conference abortive, and that the other Powers considered Russia was too important a factor in the great problem to be entirely disregarded.

He learnt that Russia was endeavouring to persuade the associated representatives that in yielding to Marmaduke's influence and in carrying out his schemes, admirable and advantageous as they might be, the Powers would be running the risk of contributing to the ambition and placing dangerous power at the disposal of one man, and thus of setting up an irresistible autocrat in place of the militarism they wished to dethrone.

A policy which Russia stigmatised in no measured terms of "jumping out of the frying-pan into the fire."

This was plausible! But Marmaduke could read between the lines. For Russia knew that the success of the conference meant the abolition of despotism in general, and Russian despotism in particular.

To give another instance of Russia's factious opposition. The representatives proposed to make the German Emperor honorary president of the conference, in recognition of the active steps he had taken towards the pacification of Europe, and the gallant sacrifice he had made in supporting the only possible preliminary to that pacification—the restoration of Alsace-Lorraine to France. This honorary presidentship was to carry with it no privileges, but was purely complimentary. The French representatives, be it said to their credit, made the proposal. No objection was advanced by any of the other representative members except those of Russia, who strenuously opposed it. As a consequence of this opposition, the proposal dropped.

Russia, in fact, meant, in as quiet and constitutional a manner as possible, to wreck the conference.

Marmaduke learnt, however, with satisfaction, that the other Powers were not inclined to submit to all Russia's demands, in case she proved too obstinate.

As his health improved, and as he continued to receive reports of stormy and unsatisfactory meetings of the conference, and frequent hitches and adjournments, he began to fret and chafe. He longed to plunge into the fray and either succeed in making the great Peace Conference a success, or die.

At last Russia threw off the mask, and, after finding that opposition and obstruction within the conference was of no further avail, finally withdrew.

But in withdrawing, the supreme moment for Russia had arrived.

In the act of withdrawing, the Government, or rather the Czar—who for Government purposes was Russia—unconsciously pulled the trigger which caused a frightful explosion—an explosion which threatened to shake the Russian Empire to its foundation and overthrow the dynasty of the Romanoffs.

Late one afternoon Marmaduke was fretting and worrying over a more than usually unsatisfactory report which he had just received, the identical report, in fact, which informed him of the withdrawal of Russia from the conference. He was sauntering near the station, when he saw, to his consternation and horror, by the staring announcements in big type on the contents bills of the evening papers, that one of the very things had happened which he had given his strength—almost his life—to prevent, viz., an eruption of brute force in the shape of a violent revolution.

He bought a *Globe*, and the startling headlines almost took away his breath. They ran:

"REVOLUTION IN RUSSIA.

"MYSTERIOUS DISAPPEARANCE OF THE CZAR.

'MEMBERS OF THE IMPERIAL FAMILY IN PRISON.

"PROVISIONAL GOVERNMENT PROCLAIMED.

"SCENES OF TERROR IN ST. PETERSBURG.

"FULL DETAILED REPORT."

He rushed to his apartments, told his landlady he must go to London by the next train, hastily packed his portmanteau, and hurried back to the station in time to catch the 6.45 p.m. up-express.

After taking his ticket, he entered the nearest first-class compartment he could see, which happened to be empty, sank into the seat, and eagerly commenced to peruse the *Globe* he had purchased.

A porter who had taken charge of his portmanteau

followed him, and placed it in the rack over his head, feeling very sore that the anticipated and customary tip was not in this instance forthcoming.

The train had just commenced to move when another passenger entered the station, hurried to the compartment in which Marmaduke was seated, flung open the door and entered. "Only just in time," he cheerily remarked to Marmaduke, who made no reply, for he was so engrossed with his *Globe* that he was perfectly oblivious to the presence of his fellow-passenger.

CHAPTER XX.

A CASE OF MISTAKEN IDENTITY PRODUCES DISASTROUS RESULTS.

WE witnessed the departure of Marmaduke for London, but before we accompany him on his journey, we must go back a few days in point of time, and introduce the reader to that popular Felixstowe institution, the extensive establishment known as the Bath Hotel.

The energetic and respected proprietor of this hotel was famed far and wide for his assiduity in providing his visitors with every possible convenience, comfort, and luxury. Hence the popularity of his establishment. On one especial point he was very popular—he spared no expense or trouble to secure the services of the very best waiters which this or any other country could produce.

Now, the worthy proprietor of the Bath Hotel congratulated himself that he possessed a perfect treasure in his head waiter, "Henri." Henri was a favourite with all the visitors, ladies as well as gentlemen, for was he not a perfect encyclopædia of information, and was he not willing, nay, eager, to give anyone and everyone the full benefit of his vast stores of knowledge? For Henri was as popular with his fellow-servants as with the visitors. Did anyone want to know anything, the cry was "Go to Henri." But information and the willingness to impart it were not Henri's only good points. Did any visitors have likes or dislikes, prejudices or predilections; Henri invariably remembered these idiosyncrasies. He always brought the right dishes and never brought the wrong ones; always remembered who liked underdone meat and who liked fat. In fact, he always waited upon each customer exactly as if the whole of the joint, the whole of the dishes and the whole of the establishment were at the exclusive disposal of that particular visitor, for the whole of the time he sojourned at the Bath Hotel.

Everyone was charmed with Henri's assiduity, Henri's knowledge, and Henri's waiting. Henri was certainly a treasure. In point of fact, Henri was a true artist in his profession.

But he was an artist in another profession besides that of a waiter! He was a professional robber! Not a common thief. Not an ordinary burglar. Not even a swell mobsman. Nevertheless a highly artistic professional robber. He himself never stole a farthing's worth of anything in his life; property was absolutely safe in his custody. But he elaborated and planned scores of robberies which were carefully executed by a select number of gentlemen, who carried out Monsieur Henri's instructions to the letter. He was the brains of the gang, and they positively adored him. Upon one point he was extremely firm. He never allowed any of the robberies he planned to be carried out in his immediate vicinity. He valued his liberty far too much to dream of allowing his pet schemes to be executed either at the Bath Hotel or even in Felixstowe. He condescended to take up his temporary abode at the Bath Hotel for two reasons. One was because he found the air of Felixstowe suited his health better than any other place which he had visited. The other was because all the year round wealthy people were invariably to be found at this particular hotel. He always felt more happy and contented when he was surrounded by wealthy people.

If but the faintest suspicion as to the real character of his treasure, Henri, had occurred to the high-minded proprietor of the famous Bath Hotel. there cannot be the slightest doubt that the shock of such a dreadful discovery would have had very serious results. Fortunately for the health of the aforesaid worthy proprietor, he firmly considered Henri was the personification of all the virtues.

One day Mr. John Saunders of 4, Little Black Street, Whitechapel — professionally known as " Gentleman Jack "—received a letter in cipher from our artistic and clever friend Henri, to the following effect :

"A. H. Morrison, diamond merchant, of 114, Hatton Garden, stopping here. Has numerous diamonds for inspection of lady client. Has expressed his intention of returning to town tomorrow (Tuesday), by 6.45 p.m. up express from Felixstowe. Only luggage, small portmanteau marked A. H. M. Come down and go by same train from Felixstowe. Secure portmanteau *en route.* Probably best spot Ipswich platform, when changing trains. Idenden shall be on Ipswich platform to render you assistance. If Morrison changes his mind and does not go by this train, stop in Felixstowe and await my instructions."

This was an excellently well-laid plan, but, like some of the best laid plans, was upset. Mr. Morrison had paid his account and ordered the hotel omnibus to take him to this train, but when Henri went to summon him, Mr. Morrison said he had changed his mind and would leave by the 10.20 train the next morning.

Henri was naturally disappointed, but thought the change of plans was of very little consequence; for he knew that when Gentleman Jack failed to see any signs of a portmanteau marked " A. H. M.," he would carry out his chief's orders, and await further instructions.

Gentleman Jack took especial care to scrutinize the passengers who alighted from the Bath Hotel omnibus. There was evidently no Mr. Morrison and certainly no " A. H. M." portmanteau, for there stepped down from the omnibus, on its arrival at the station, a very old lady and a little girl, and no luggage whatever. Gentleman Jack, however, kept a strict watch over all arrivals. He was soon rewarded by seeing a gentleman hurry into the booking office at the last moment, carrying in his hand a small portmanteau, upon which was painted " A. H. M." in plain block letters, which could easily have been read by the youngest pupil in the neighbouring board school who knew his or her A B C.

"Oh!" mentally ejaculated Gentleman Jack; "walked instead of rode, I suppose. Looks rather worried. Perhaps he feels troubled about taking care of his diamonds. Well, I'll do my best to relieve him of that trouble."

A porter took the portmanteau from the hand of the supposed Mr. Morrison, who took his ticket, and then proceeded to enter an empty first-class compartment, as the reader is already aware; followed by Gentleman Jack.

Now Gentleman Jack never dreamt for one moment that the passenger he saw was any other than Mr. A. H. Morrison; or that the portmanteau marked "A. H. M." was any other than the particular portmanteau regarding which he had received his chief's instructions.

It has already been related how Marmaduke was so occupied with his newspaper that he ignored the greeting of his companion.

The train had just drawn out of Felixstowe station when Gentleman Jack made another attempt to start a conversation.

"I am afraid that stupid porter placed your portmanteau in rather a tottery position; let me adjust it for you."

Again Marmaduke ignored the remark. He was eagerly perusing *The Globe*, and was evidently oblivious to everything but the newspaper before him. He was deeply engrossed in what he was reading, for he bent his head lower and lower and steadied his newspaper on his knees.

Gentleman Jack, somewhat like his chief, was a genius, although of an inferior type. Given an outline plan, he possessed that peculiar ability which enabled him, when the appropriate time came, to fill in the details of that plan with remarkable rapidity and accuracy.

He knew that this express train ran through to Ipswich without stopping; at the same time the whole distance was not far, and he knew that whatever he decided to do must be done quickly. In a moment his plans were formed. Perhaps the bent head of the victim helped the formation of those plans. The miscreant put his hand in his pocket, drew forth a small, heavy life-preserver, and raised his hand to strike his victim's bowed head. Just then Marmaduke mechanically raised his head and saw the uplifted hand. But before he had time to raise a finger or stir a muscle in his defence, the cruel blow had descended on the top of his head, and Marmaduke fell forward senseless!

Now, Gentleman Jack regarded his acts from a professional standpoint. He never desired to cause injury to anyone. He regretted the necessity to injure anyone. At the same time, if in carrying out his professional duty of robbing anyone, that person sustained an injury—well, so much the worse for the robbee. As to sentiment and feeling, Gentleman Jack never allowed these awkward characteristics to impede him in the execution of what he considered his professional duty.

It follows, therefore, that whenever he had occasion to knock his victim senseless, or even (quite accidentally) to kill him, Gentleman Jack was by no means agitated. He was not even flurried.

In such an emergency, therefore, as the present one, he was perfectly calm and collected. Had he lost his head, he would have considered himself, professionally, disgraced.

He first drew down the blinds on both sides of the carriage. Then he proceeded deliberately and rapidly to rifle his victim's pockets. He abstracted first the watch, then the purse, then a bulky pocket book. While extracting the latter, he noticed a thin gold chain round the unconscious man's neck. This chain the robber pulled off, and to it he found attached a curious kind of medal. However, he had no time to examine any of these, but hurriedly put the chain round his neck and thrust the remainder of the articles into his capacious pockets.

The time occupied from the moment of stunning the unfortunate victim until his pockets were completely emptied was incredibly short. Shorter, in fact, than the time occupied in telling the tale.

The next point was what to do with the body.

The robber lifted one of the blinds and looked out of the window.

The train was rapidly leaving Trimley Station lights a good distance in the rear, and so far as the darkness enabled him to determine, Trimley Street and the scattered cottages in the vicinity had been passed, and they had reached the open country just opposite the cross road which leads to the Trimley Board School. He then drew his victim to the near side of the carriage farthest away from the Felixstowe road which runs parallel with the railway, cautiously opened the carriage door, kept himself out of sight as much as possible, and thrust the unconscious man out of the carriage.

There was very little sound beyond a slight thud, as the body reached the ground. It rolled over and over out of sight, and the train sped on in the darkness.

CHAPTER XXI.

"THE GOOD SAMARITAN" IN THE GUISE OF A FARM LABOURER.

NOT far from the spot where, and at the identical time when, poor Marmaduke was bundled so unceremoniously from the train, there happened to be a farm labourer at work. Even such hard-driven men as farm labourers do not usually work late in the evening after dark. But in the present instance this particular farm labourer, John Chapman, residing at Falkenham, first horseman on a neighbouring farm—a man who will play an important part in this history—was about to cart some straw for his employer from a farm near the railway.

Chapman had just drawn his cart up to the strawstack, and was about to load the straw, when the train rattled by. The man raised his head to look at it, for sights, even a passing train, were not to be despised by the folk of sleepy, out-of-the-world Falkenham.

The lights of the carriages were sharply silhouetted against the background of the darkness, and the man was intently watching these pretty lights when he was startled to see one of the carriage doors suddenly swing open and a man fall headlong out.

"Treacherous things, them carriage doors," muttered Chapman, as he ran as well as he could towards the spot where he saw the man fall. "I wonder there ain't more people tumble out o' trains through careless porters leaving doors unfastened. I'll be bound to say as it's that Bill Mais as never fastened the door at Felixstowe. He's been fined a'ready for the same thing to my knowledge."

When Chapman arrived at the line he could see no appearance of the fallen man. He had evidently miscalculated the spot. However, after searching for a few moments, and guided by some slight groans, he found the unfortunate man in the middle of some bushes, huddled in a heap, evidently only a few yards from where he fell.

Chapman was a man of action rather than words. "Poor gentleman," said he, as he dimly distinguished the inanimate heap before him, "he have had a nasty tumble. I must do what I can for him."

The first thing to be done was to run back to where he left the cart, put some straw at the bottom of it, and bring the horse and cart to the spot, which could also be done without difficulty. Then he lifted the man, who was still groaning piteously, into the cart. Then, carefully leading the horse, and avoiding ruts and stones as well as he could, he made his way to Trimley Street, and stopped at the door of Dr. Smith.

He gave a lusty pull at the bell, and in a few moments a middle-aged woman, the doctor's servant, housekeeper, and factotum, Margaret, opened the door. The visitor told his tale in a very few words.

"Oh, dear, dear, Mr. Chapman," said the housekeeper, "it's no use bringing the poor man here; the doctor went to Woodbridge early this afternoon to attend a terrible serious case, and I don't know when he'll be back. All the Felixstowe and Walton doctors were out, or you may be sure the people wouldn't have come here. I wouldn't have gone if I had been him. It's a mortal wonder how Dr. Smith is put upon, and as good a one any day as those Felixstowe fellows."

Margaret was a firm believer in the skill and ability of her master, and was always very firm in upholding what she considered his professional rights.

"But what shall I do, Margaret? You can hear the poor man groan now."

"Do you take him straight to the Ipswich Hospital, Mr. Chapman; it's no use waiting for the doctor. Like enough he won't be back for hours."

Just then the tramp of a galloping horse was heard. It was evidently galloping furiously. It came rapidly nearer and nearer, and in a few minutes the animal was pulled up, almost on its haunches, at the doctor's door. The rider saw the open door and the doctor's housekeeper standing there talking to a man. Without alighting, he leaned over the low fence in front of the house and called out: "Dr. Smith is wanted at once at Orwell Station. There has been a fearful accident, and lots of people are injured. Send him up there at once. I am going on to get carriages to take the injured to the East Suffolk Hospital. I reckon the nurses there will be pretty well occupied. It'll be pretty full in an hour or so."

Without waiting for a reply from his astonished audience, he lashed his horse and galloped on towards Walton.

"Well, here's a pretty kettle of fish," said Chapman. "What with one thing and another, I feel as if I was wholly dawzled. What shall I do now?"

Woman's wits then, as ever, were equal to the emergency.

"Look you here, Master Chapman," said Margaret, "this poor gentleman won't get much attention at the hospital to-night. Do you take him straight to your home; your wife can nurse him as well as anybody. You mind the time you fell off that stover stack last year, and Dr. Smith said she was as good as a professional nurse. And I'll promise you this: directly the doctor comes back from Woodbridge, he shan't go anywhere before he comes to you."

Chapman saw that, under the circumstances, this was the best thing to do, especially as the sooner the injured man received some kind of attention the better.

With a hasty parting word of admonition to Margaret "to be sure and send the doctor directly he arrived," Chapman soon led his horse in the direction of his home.

Mrs. Chapman was in the cosy living room of her little cottage near Falkenham Street, waiting for the return of her husband. She was busy with some domestic duty while she was waiting; for Mrs. Chapman was an industrious body, and could always find plenty to occupy her hands. So industrious was she that she would have been ashamed to sit with her hands before her, even if her ordinary routine of daily toil was done. Presently, hearing the tramp of the horse, and recognising her husband's footsteps as only a wife, and a loving wife, can recognise them, she went to the door and opened it.

A very few words sufficed to inform her that he had brought an injured man home. She waited for no details, but set about helping her husband carry the helpless man into the house, up the narrow staircase, and into the bedroom, over the living room.

While they were engaged in getting him as comfortably settled as they possibly could on the bed— they hesitated to undress him till the doctor arrived —the good wife gathered some of the particulars of her husband's story.

"Poor dear, poor dear," she muttered, "how ill he do look."

"Yes," responded Chapman, "I see the door fling open as distinctly as I see you now, and he simply tumbled clean out. He must have been leaning on the door and took quite unawares, for he never so much as shruk, but come straight down, and when I found him he was all of a heap among the whins. I hope to goodness the bushes broke his fall."

"He don't seem to have any bruises or cuts about him, only some scratches," interpolated the wife. "Hullo! what's this, a big bruise on the top of the head. He have had a nasty knock. Depend upon it that's what's done the mischief. He must have fell with his head against the step of the carriage, or on a stone or piece of iron or something."

Meantime the worthy couple did what their common sense and such experience as they possessed dictated. Neither Chapman nor his wife had ever attended any lectures upon first aid to the wounded, nor did they ever belong to any ambulance class, but for all that they did a good many things for which the doctor afterwards praised them. At any rate, without their kind and prompt help it would undoubtedly have gone very hard with poor Marmaduke.

Doctor Smith returned from Woodbridge sooner than was expected, and, true to the promise made by his housekeeper on his behalf, went straight to Chapman's cottage. He examined the injured man, who still remained unconscious, and soon reported to the anxious couple who awaited his diagnosis, that no bones were broken, and, save and except the one nasty blow on the head, no injuries had been sustained, barring a few minor contusions and scratches. "Except for this one blow," said the doctor, "the man has escaped injury by a miracle. All you can do is to follow the instructions I have already given you, and I will call and see him again to-morrow. We must hope that in a short time he will regain consciousness. If he does he will probably recover."

They then searched for any clue by which he could be identified, but they could find none. They found in his pocket a bunch of keys, a first class single ticket from Felixstowe to Liverpool Street, a pocket-handkerchief, a roll of Bank of England notes, and some loose gold and silver. His linen was marked " A. H." He was evidently a gentleman. But there was nothing upon him by which they could discover who he was, or where he came from.

The doctor said he must not be moved for the present, so Chapman and his wife had no option but to keep the injured man in their cottage, do the best they could for him, and trust to his speedy return to consciousness, so that they might advise his friends.

An hour or so after Marmaduke had been placed comfortably in bed and attended to by the doctor, he seemed to wake up, but it was only to a semi-conscious state. He took the nourishment which was offered to him, but could neither speak nor understand when spoken to. He continued in this condition for several days, sleeping at intervals.

It was late in the afternoon of the fifth day after he had been brought to Falkenham, that he opened his eyes and woke to full consciousness as from a dream.

At first he wondered what had happened to him. He rubbed his eyes to ascertain if he was really awake. Then he remembered the uplifted hand, the last thing he had seen before the blow rendered him unconscious, and wondered why he was not in the railway carriage, for, of course, the intervening time was blank to him.

He sat up and looked round. The room was small, the walls were whitewashed, the window was a tiny one, and the panes in it were tiny in proportion.

There was no carpet on the floor, and no fireplace in the room. A small square hole in the floor formed the head of the straight ladder-like staircase which led from a room below. The bed upon which he lay was on a small, plain iron bedstead, devoid of hangings or drapery. What little furniture the room contained was evidently very old and well worn, but everything was very clean. The floor boards were very white and extremely furrowed, quite as much from frequent and energetic scrubbing as from old age or wear.

"Where can I be?" muttered Marmaduke. "It was only a minute ago that I felt that miscreant knock me on the head. Yet here am I undressed and in bed. It was a mercy he didn't kill me. I feel rather stiff, and my head throbs a little, but otherwise I am all right. Where can I be?"

He again glanced round the room, "Ha, there are some newspapers on a chair. They look recent ones. Perhaps the dates upon them will throw some light on the matter." The chair was by the side of the bed. He leaned forward and took up the papers. They were copies of *The East Anglian Daily Times*. The first one was dated the day after he entered the train to leave Felixstowe. The next one bore the succeeding day's date. But what did this deep black border round the edge of the paper mean? Marmaduke turned to the back page of the paper where the latest news is always to be found, and there he saw some big black head-lines which burnt themselves into his brain, and made him feel giddy and faint.

The most prominent of these head-lines ran:

"THE TERRIBLE RAILWAY ACCIDENT.

"Tragic Death of Marmaduke.

"Discovery of his Dead Body amongst the Debris.

"Full Details."

The paper dropped from his hands and he fell back again on the bed just as the head of Mrs. Chapman appeared, rising above the floor of the staircase.

CHAPTER XXII.

HOW MARMADUKE READS A CATEGORICAL AND CIRCUMSTANTIAL ACCOUNT OF HIS OWN DEATH.

DIRECTLY Mrs. Chapman entered the room she saw by the papers on the bed, as well as the look of intelligence in her patient's eyes as they followed her about, that he had regained his mental powers.

Although this was what she expected and hoped for, she was yet taken by surprise and scarcely knew what to say. The patient was the first to break the silence.

"I perceive, my good woman, that I am in excellent hands; but I should like to know where I am, and how it is I am here."

"I am real glad you've come to yourself, sir; and I can very soon tell you how it is you're here. Last Tuesday my husband he came home much later than usual to tea, and he say 'Mother, I've got to take 'Smiler' and the light tumbrel down to Trimley to cart some straw for master. He say he must have it to-night; so, mother,' says he, 'let's have a cup of tea, quick, and I'm off.'"

Mrs. Chapman was rather voluble and did not possess the knack of condensing either her remarks or her information. She told her story, it is true, but she was compelled to unroll it from her brain at a very slow rate, otherwise she could not unroll it at all. However, by the exercise of a certain amount of patience, and after putting a few judicious questions, her listener ascertained how he was seen to tumble from the train, what had befallen him since, and gathered that he was practically indebted to the honest couple for his present existence.

"There, sir, I think I have told you all I know, but my husband won't be long; perhaps he can tell you more. Why there he is just come in. Come up here, Chapman," she called out in a louder tone; "the gentleman he have come to himself and wants to see you."

Chapman slowly ascended the stairs, came across to the bed, and stood by the side of his wife, who, at her patient's request, had seated herself in a chair.

Marmaduke saw before him a man who had left youth and middle age behind him; who had a bent, very bent form, sharp features, bright sparkling eyes, and black hair, which curled naturally. Whether his wife, whom he affectionately called "mother," had ever been a handsome woman in her youth, we cannot say. Hard work had left its indelible stamp on face and form. But work had not been able to obliterate from her features that pleasing attractiveness which a kind heart, a good temper, and a desire to help those around invariably impart to features the most homely. Chapman told the tale over again, with his own variations, and a few, very few, additions; but before he had quite finished his wife interrupted him:

"There, Chapman, you had better not talk any more. The doctor say the gentleman must be kept quiet, and must not be excited. When you feel a little stronger, sir, we should like to know where to send to your friends. They are sure to be anxious about you, and there are some papers which you can read when you're able, that will show you that your tumble out of the train was providential, and what a miraculous escape you had from being killed in a fearful railway accident."

Now up to this time Marmaduke had no more idea of shirking his duty by remaining hidden or concealing his identity, than he had of committing suicide or giving any other indication of insanity. But having satisfied himself of his whereabouts, and that he was in safe hands, he considered it only judicious, before he gave any information as to his identity, to investigate the astounding report which he had noticed in the papers as to his death and the discovery of his body. He therefore thanked Chapman and his wife most warmly for their great kindness to him in his extremity, told them that they might rest content that at present no one would be anxious on his account, and said he would rather await his entire recovery before disturbing any of his friends. He then shut his eyes, and said he would like to remain quiet and alone for an hour or two. His homely nurse brought him some nourishment, smoothed his pillows, made him comfortable, admonished him to "keep quiet and rest his poor head," and then left him for a time. He kept his eyes shut for a quarter of an hour, and then commenced to examine the newspapers.

The first he opened was a copy of *The East Anglian Daily Times* for Wednesday, the day after he started on his eventful journey.

The following are portions of what he read :—

"FEARFUL RAILWAY ACCIDENT AT ORWELL.

"Great Loss of Life.

"Terrible Scenes.

"A terrible accident occurred last evening to the 6.45 p.m. up express train from Felixstowe. As our readers are aware, this train runs through from Felixstowe to Ipswich without stopping, and is timed to catch the 7.17 up train from Ipswich.

"The Felixstowe Railway has a single line only, but the rails are doubled at all the stations, so that trains going in opposite directions can pass one another.

"It appears that the ill-fated train proceeded safely until it reached Orwell Station. Here an up goods train had been shunted on to the down line in order to let the express pass. When, however, the passenger train entered the station, the facing points, either from the result of some carelessness or accident—which will have to be the subject of the most stringent investigation—had been wrongly placed, and the passenger train dashed into the rear of the stationary goods train. In accordance with the usual regulations the train 'slowed' before entering the station, but unfortunately the speed was sufficiently high to cause a portion of both trains to be completely wrecked. The passenger engine mounted upon a number of the rear trucks and reduced them to fragments. The guard's van and several of the carriages 'telescoped' and fell to pieces, and hardly a carriage of the moving train escaped without some injury.

"A collision of this character *per se* would have been sufficiently terrible, but another horror was added to the scene. Three of the rear trucks into which the engine dashed were filled with casks of petroleum, which had been landed the day before from a barque at Felixstowe quay, and were in course of transit to London. A number of the casks were shattered to pieces, and the furnace of the engine set the petroleum on fire. Nearly the whole of the passenger carriages were at once enveloped in flames. The result was too horrible to contemplate. The heap of *débris*, the roaring of the flames, the occasional explosion of a barrel of petroleum, the groans of the injured, the shrieks of the uninjured passengers unable to escape from the burning carriages, were sights and sounds so agonizing that they will never be forgotten by the few people at Orwell Station who happened to be spectators. Assistance was out of the question. The flames burnt so fiercely and the volumes of smoke which arose were so suffocating, that for some time no one could approach the scene. It is to be hoped that death soon put an end to the sufferings of the unhappy victims. Not a single one of the ill-fated passengers in the first three carriages escaped. All were either burnt or suffocated to death. Besides these, many persons in the succeeding carriages received fearful injuries.

* * * * * *

"As we go to press we learn that the flames have abated, and that gangs of railway labourers are employed in removing the *débris* and conveying the charred remains of the unfortunate passengers to the station-master's house for identification, where such is possible. In many cases features are unrecognisable, and great difficulty will, therefore, be experienced in identifying many of the bodies."

* * * * * *

The next paper which Marmaduke examined was the one upon which appeared the deep black border, and bore the following day's date. Under the startling headlines already given, he read the following:

"In our issue of yesterday we recorded that the semi-burnt bodies of the victims of the terrible railway disaster were being recovered from the *débris* and conveyed to the station-master's house. Yesterday was occupied in the attempt to identify some of these bodies. One of the first to be examined was the wholly unrecognisable remains of a man. One of the railway officials happened to see attached to a fine semi-fused chain which had evidently been worn, and was even then tightly clasped round the neck of the deceased, a medal. Upon brushing the dust from this medal, there could be clearly deciphered, the words, 'To Marmaduke, from his affectionate friend, Wilhelm.' At first, it was considered incredible that the remains could be those of that renowned man. The news spread like wildfire, the telegraph was put into requisition, and a special train speedily brought down several friends of Marmaduke from the Foreign Office and the German Embassy, and a staff of detectives. The melancholy intelligence was soon placed beyond a doubt. It was ascertained that Marmaduke left his apartments at Martello House for the purpose of catching the ill-fated 6.45 express. He took his portmanteau with him. He was traced to the station and seen to take his ticket. A porter carried his portmanteau into a first-class compartment, saw him enter it, and asserts that he was still seated in it when the train left Felixstowe. The identical portmanteau, partially consumed, but containing papers closely wrapped together, which could still be clearly identified, was found in close proximity to the supposed corpse of Marmaduke. Moreover, the gold watch and chain engraved with the deceased's name, which watch he was always known to carry, was found upon the remains. It had evidently been worn at the time of the accident, for although the clothes were burnt, the watch and chain had been forced between the calcined ribs of the charred body. If further evidence of the identity of the deceased were required, this evidence was established by the purse containing several identifiable articles, and also a charred pocket-book, containing several recognisable objects, all closely adhering to the charred body of the deceased.

"It is established beyond the possibility of a doubt that Marmaduke, undoubtedly the foremost man in Europe at the present time, was tragically killed in the fearful railway accident which occurred at Orwell Station the night before last. As will be seen by the foreign telegrams in another portion of our issue, there is not a capital in Europe which is not profoundly moved by this terrible catastrophe."

* * * * * *

After a short rest he looked through the remaining copies of *The East Anglian Daily Times*, which the thoughtful Chapman had placed on the chair.

There were many other details which the sick man read, but they gave no more information than was contained in the extracts which we have already given.

Just as he was about to place the newspapers back on the chair and rest his weary brain, he caught sight of an article in that day's newspaper, extracted from *The Times* of the previous day, which, when he had glanced through it, caused him inaudibly to thank God that he had not divulged his identity to honest Chapman and his wife.

CHAPTER XXIII.

HOW AN ESCRITOIRE WAS BROKEN OPEN IN THE "TELEPHONE ROOM" OF THE IMPERIAL PALACE IN BERLIN, AND WHAT WAS DISCOVERED THEREIN.

WE must now ask the reader to take an Asmodean flight to Berlin. The whole of Germany was stunned to receive the news of the tragic death of Marmaduke. From the Emperor to his humblest subject the whole nation seemed as if it had received a crushing blow. To say that the nation mourned is to convey but a feeble idea of the feelings which actuated the whole of the German people. But it is not of the grief of individuals or of communities, it is not of elaborate funeral ceremonies, it is not of the weeping of a nation, that we wish to speak now.

Let us enter the luxuriously furnished Telephone Room in the Imperial Palace. It looks exactly the same as it did when we witnessed the interview between the Emperor and Marmaduke, when it was decided that the latter should undertake the memorable mission to the French people. Again the room has two occupants. The Emperor is standing erect, silent, sad, stern, with arms folded. He is closely watching a workman, who is engaged in attempting to pick the lock of the massive escritoire. The man tries several skeleton keys and other tools, but the lock refuses to yield.

The Emperor grows impatient. "Never mind; break it open."

The man employs stronger tools, and the lock is forcibly wrenched from its place.

"That will do. You can retire." The door closes and the Emperor is alone. He takes hold of the handle of the drawer, pauses a few moments, and allows a sigh to escape him, for the Emperor mourns for a lost friend. That piece of furniture held Marmaduke's private papers; no one else had access to it. What does it contain? Mere trifles, relics of the past, cherished letters, or documents of weightier interest? At last the Emperor's reverie abruptly terminates. He pulls open the front of the escritoire, wheels a comfortable lounge in front of it, seats himself, and proceeds in a very deliberate manner to examine the contents of the various compartments and drawers before him.

There are a number of papers, letters, rough drafts, and sundry memoranda, all arranged in exquisite order.

Almost the first thing touched was an envelope containing a lock of brown hair. On the outside of the envelope was pencilled the word "Avis."

Then came some sheets of music, evidently original compositions. One was a chorale on the well-known hymn, "It came upon the midnight clear." The melody to which the first four verses were set was in a minor key. In the last verse, in which is recited the fulfilment of the glorious golden age of peace, the minor gave place to the major, and a joyous burst of melody ensued.

Pinned to this chorale was an anthem on the words:

> "Christ is risen, is risen from the dead. Hallelujah. Glory to God in the highest, and on earth peace, good will towards men."

The anthem concluded with Hallelujah and Amen choruses. There were numerous notes and memoranda—some mere jottings of fugitive ideas, some very rough and incomplete. All were suggestive, even when they were not very coherent, or even logical. For instance :

"Grand secret. To solve every abstruse problem, to answer every difficult question, whether social, political, or personal, apply to it the Christianity of Christ.

"Grand object. To divert legislation and political action from the subsidiary channels of self-interest, class interest, party interest, to central channels of rightness, brotherhood, love.

"If principles are right, and they are rightly applied, result must be right.

"Rightness must ultimately spell success. Rightness is the policy that pays, and that gives the greatest happiness to the greatest number.

"Convertible terms—Fatherhood of God, brotherhood of man.

"Highest ideal—To see the will of God done on earth as it is done in heaven.

"While Christianity in its purity, the Christianity of Christ (note, not necessarily the Christianity of the creeds or the churches) is academically accepted, it is practically rejected, especially when we come to the domains of politics and diplomacy. But the time is coming—must come—when the result of what I may term the 'rebirth' of this pure Christianity, will be that monarchs, governments, and peoples will take it as their paramount and guiding principle.

"There are forces too frequently lost sight of by governments and rulers. Forces far more powerful than all material forces. In the immediate future, armies, political parties, and monarchs must condescend to recognise and deal with moral and spiritual forces.

"The spiritual is infinitely superior to the physical, and in the former I recognise the ultimate solvent of that terrible question—militarism and brute force.

"All so absurdly simple, so self evident.

"Peoples and statesmen accept them in the abstract and reject them in the concrete, recognise them in print and disown them in action.

"Query. How to reverse all this."

The Emperor smiled sardonically when he read the following :—

> "Many Socialists look upon me with suspicion because I uphold the monarchical principle, but to do so is not only advantageous but necessary. Up to a certain point monarchy forms a splendid counterbalance weight to democracy, and is an important factor in preserving the equilibrium of good government. It is possible for the democratic principle, as well as the monarchical principle, to be abused, in which case either will become intolerable."

Frequently Marmaduke was philosophical in his jottings, but whether philosophical, political, or social, he always managed to return to his one predominant point—" righteousness."

"I once saw this motto quoted 'Systema omnia vincit,' but I think I can improve upon it—'Righteousness *plus* Method conquer the world.'"

But although Marmaduke was not quite prepared to accept the motto "Systema omnia vincit," yet he systematised everything with which he had to deal in an extraordinary and exhaustive manner. He had the natural gift of organisation, and he was careful to highly develop that gift.

The imperial reader patiently waded through the pile of papers, making sundry notes and comments here and there upon the margins of the documents.

There were elaborate and carefully classified calculations and tables regarding disarmament, showing how it could be most advantageously carried out by each nation.

He showed *(a)* that disarmament must be gradual, so that soldiers may be absorbed into civil life without producing those commercial disasters which would ensue, if enormous numbers of soldiers were suddenly turned adrift.

Then he showed *(b)* how disarmament would enable taxation to be enormously reduced, and by exactly how much, and yet leave a sufficient margin for a fund to enable numerous pressing reforms to be carried out.

In these notes he displayed such a profound knowledge of discipline, routine, and military matters generally, that one would almost feel inclined to believe he had spent years upon the headquarter staff of each of the great European armies.

Connected with, and, of course, dependent upon these military calculations and suggestions, were notes giving every possible detail regarding the taxation of each country. There were also elaborate tabular statements, and analyses of those statements, showing the financial results in each country if the projected disarmament were carried out. Of subsidiary topics, free trade was one. Marmaduke showed that protective tariffs were simply means employed by one nation for endeavouring to obtain undue commercial advantage over another nation, but without succeeding in doing so. The suicidal policy of protection put him in mind of the old policy of "cutting off one's nose to be revenged on one's face."

Amongst numerous letters and draft replies the following will show the trend of Marmaduke's mind and thought. It was a rough draft of a letter to a nobleman, but to whom was unknown, for the name was not given.

> "My dear Count,—Many thanks for your kind and sympathetic letter. You assume that I shall be 'overwhelmed and crushed with the gigantic task of elaborating a system of political and social reform for such a vast area as Europe.' What would you say if I told you that in dealing with Europe and European questions, I had a difficult task to persuade myself that I was not contemplating the infinitely little under a microscope?

"Listen! The other day I was reading for my amusement about a star known as No. 1,830 in Groombridge's catalogue. This star is invisible to the naked eye, and is supposed to be ten times as far from the solar system as Alpha Centauri, the sun's nearest neighbour. 1,830 Groombridge appears to be rushing through space at the rate of 200 miles a second. Now about twenty-five miles a second seems to be the maximum rate at which a star must move in order to be kept by attraction within the limits of our sidereal system. It follows, therefore, that 1,830 Groombridge is beyond the influence of our system, and must be a mere passing visitor, coming from space beyond our ken, and journeying to space beyond our ken. So that, after all, the sidereal system we know of (comprising about one hundred million stars) must merely be a small corner in the universe!

"After amusing myself for an hour in this manner, I resumed my work—the investigation of the infinitely little under a microscope.

"Yours very sincerely,
"MARMADUKE."

But what most attracted the attention of the Emperor was a bulky set of papers, upon the top sheet of which was written:

"REPORT UPON PROPOSED INTERNATIONAL REFORMS FOR EUROPE.

"To be produced in case the conference arrives at a preliminary agreement."

Upon the next sheet was the following :

"Countries differ, races differ, habits and customs differ, and these varied conditions naturally necessitate different treatment, but the principles of Christianity will be found sufficiently elastic to apply to all these variations."

Then came the report. Although it was lengthy, there was not a word too much. It was written in the concisest terms, yet not a point was omitted, and every point was perfectly clear.

Certainly Marmaduke had taken enormous trouble and displayed wonderful skill and knowledge in preparing this report.

Every possible and imaginable point had been touched upon, lucidly treated, and relegated to its proper position. National prejudices were not forgotten. Racial and geographical distinctions and differences received their proper share of notice. Minor points and collateral issues had due attention given to them. Each question which arose was answered, and each problem encountered was solved. And answer and solution were strongly fortified by unanswerable arguments and carefully collated statistics.

He did not commit the fatal blunder of moulding the administration of every country after a cast-iron pattern. Plenty of room was left for individual efforts, individual idiosyncrasies, and individual progress. Existing laws and existing constitutions, as well as the habits and customs of each country, were not interfered with so long as they did not hinder progress and were not productive of injustice or oppression. Admirable checks were suggested for ensuring administrative purity, impartial justice, and equality of treatment of persons of different religions.

The principles were clearly enunciated which should govern the just and equitable annexation of new territory or the creation of protectorates or spheres of influence. At the same time, ample scope was left for peaceful and commercial expansion and development, and for the due exercise of whatever powers of colonization each nation possessed.

Conditions were suggested by which it was rendered impossible for a number of powerful nations to exhibit the "dog in the manger" policy of standing guard over some unfortunate maladministered oppressed country, which all these nations desired, but which none would suffer the other to possess; whilst, as a consequence of this international jealousy, the maladministration remained unaltered, and the oppression was unchecked.

Means were also devised for ensuring absolute protection to subject races, both as regards their existing rights and future development. All questions of international interest, whether social, political, or religious, received due notice.

The safeguards which he suggested for preventing the Bund itself from degenerating into an irresponsible autocracy were extremely simple; at the same time they were as ingenious as they were effectual. That terrific explosive "Queljanite," under the touch of Marmaduke, was transformed from a perpetual menace of war to one of the chief factors in maintaining peace.

Each line of this report indicated extreme care and concentration of thought and knowledge. But if in any portion of it the writer could be said to surpass himself, it was in that section which dealt with the methods and suggestions for promoting permanent peace and preventing the possibility of war.

Means were devised for ensuring that the principles of conciliation and mediation, and, if these failed, of arbitration, should be brought to bear upon all disputes, no matter of what nature, whether social, commercial, political, or international.

The whole was not only most carefully and accurately, but exhaustively thought out. In fact, the draught clauses, the suggestions, the memoranda, the tables, the statistics, the arguments, and the explanations contained in this report, practically formed a comprehensive constitution for Europe—an effective European Bund—a continent of allies.

Finally, by the terms of this constitution, Marmaduke effectually put it out of the power of ambition, revenge, jingoism, or sheer obstinacy, of either sovereigns, courts, governments, or even peoples, to wage in future an aggressive war. For a government or a nation to declare such a war against any other nation, meant the absolute certainty of a combination of all the other associated Powers, against the aggressor and in defence of the nation attacked.

CHAPTER XXIV.

A LITTLE COTTAGE AT FALKENHAM AND ITS INMATES.

WE will now return to the bedside of the injured man. The following are extracts from *The Times* article which attracted Marmaduke's attention, and caused him to be thankful that he had not divulged his identity. It was headed—

"EFFECT OF MARMADUKE'S DEATH UPON EUROPEAN POLITICS.

"It is not too much to assert that Europe mourns. When a great and good king or statesmen dies, the particular nation to which he belongs knows that it has sustained a crushing blow in the loss of a near friend, and a dear one. But in the perspective of geographical distance, other nations, although they may mourn, are apt to regard the lost one merely as a newspaper acquaintance, and a distant one at that. With Marmaduke it is different. His death is regarded as a personal loss equally to Anglo-Saxon, Teuton, or Gaul. The disaster is not merely national, it is international.

"He is mourned by the nations of Europe collectively as well as severally, as a tribune of the people, and as an international champion of peace, equity, justice, and righteousness. England has the honour of claiming him by birth, but the whole of Europe claims him by right of the stronger bond of sympathy and love.

* * * * * *

"We have all sustained a grievous blow. But we must not lose heart. Providence has already begun to shape the ends of this apparently irreparable disaster.

"There is no use in disguising the fact that up to the time of the death of this truly great man, there existed an uneasy feeling amongst most European governments, regarding what may be termed the personal question. Expression was first given to this uneasiness by a government known to be hostile to him, and such uneasiness was fostered, strangely enough, by his known rigid adherence to the monarchical principle. The disquietude consisted in the feeling that there was a possibility, remote perhaps, but still a possibility, that the time might come when Marmaduke would conceivably be inclined to work for his own hand. Given latent ambition, a mental twist, a combination of unforeseen circumstances, and Europe might wake up, when it was too late, to the fact that she was face to face with one of the most powerful and dangerous autocrats this world had ever seen.

"Of course, with the death of Marmaduke this uneasiness vanishes.

* * * * * *

"The telegrams we publish to-day from our correspondents in Berlin, Paris, Vienna, Brussels, Rome, and even New York, indicate a remarkable unanimity. They all agree that had Marmaduke lived, the opposition he would have encountered first and last might have been insurmountable. They all agree, moreover, and here the agreement is more remarkable still, that now he is dead, the crucial objections to his policy will fall to the ground, and there is every possibility that the reforms for which he laboured so hard will ultimately be carried out.

"If it were possible for the dead man to read these lines, he would rejoice that death in his case has probably made all the difference between the rejection and adoption of his most cherished schemes.

"The world is longing for peace, longing for rest, longing for freedom from the harass of militarism, longing for the new *régime*. By the irony of fate, the death of the chief advocate of these long wished for reforms has rendered their adoption, and that in the immediate future, a glorious possibility."

* * * * * *

Marmaduke was recovering, although slowly. He had lodged with the worthy couple for several weeks, and was being nursed back to health by them with all the capacity they possessed. He still refrained from divulging his identity. They knew from his linen that his initials were A. H., so pending his decision as to his future course of action he took the maiden name of his mother, and called himself Arthur Hamilton.

Fortunately he had enough ready cash for his wants in the immediate future. He was therefore able to ponder over the strange events which had happened, and what he proposed to do.

Falkenham and its surroundings were eminently fitted for meditation.

He found, when he was sufficiently recovered to leave his room and take a walk, that Chapman's cottage was a cosy little four-roomed brick building. On one side, that facing the road, it had a small, plain entrance-door, one small window on the ground floor, and one small window on the first floor. There was only one chimney-stack to the house, and on this side the bricks were tarred black. From this point of view it could certainly not be described as picturesque, for it was essentially commonplace and prosaic. Some people might have called it ugly.

As seen from the other side, however, the little cottage was more presentable (see frontispiece). This side boasted of four windows, one for each room. All the windows were of the casement type, and one of them, that which gave light to the living room, was quite a grand window in comparison to its tiny companions, for it possessed two mullions instead of one, and was of a true Early English type, for it was cut up into eighteen small panes, and was considerably broader than it was high. On one side of the back door stood a low, long settle or stool, upon which rested some pails and cans. And upon the doorstep sat Mrs. Chapman's pet cat, winking and blinking in the sun, and looking thoroughly at home, as if she and not her master were the legal and responsible tenant of the little cottage. This little cottage stood by the side of a road which in one direction led to Falkenham village and the main Ipswich road, and in the other direction wandered on through a part of the village known by the unprepossessing name of Falkenham Sink, and finally lost itself in marshes on the banks of the Deben. It is not at all surprising that, situated as it was, at some distance from the railway, away from the main road, the tiny village of Falkenham was quiet, excessively quiet. Some persons of a malicious temperament might even have called it sleepy.

The only lions of the locality appeared to be the interesting old church of S. Ethelbert, built in the reign of Richard III., and a particularly prosperous farmer. But even these lions were not very formidable when viewed even from the next village, much less from the nearest market-town.

In any case Marmaduke found very little to interrupt him when he took a walk and wished to meditate, except when he came across one of the few farmers of the neighbourhood, a labourer or two at work in the fields, or some of the village children, with whom he soon became friends and was very popular.

When, however, he wished to ensure exceptional solitude, he would walk across the marshes to the Deben and follow the river wall till he reached the mouth at Bawdsey. During this walk of three miles out and three miles home he never met anyone, except on two occasions—once when he came across a jolly, good-tempered man, who was said to be the guardian of the river wall, and once when he lost his way on the marshes and was put in the right path and carried across more than one of the numerous intersecting ditches by honest John Utteridge, tenant of "The Falkenham Dog."

Falkenham was certainly a very secluded spot, but Marmaduke found that quite as much news of the outer world as he desired was filtered to him through the convenient channel of *The East Anglian Daily Times*.

However picturesque, delightful, and bracing he found his walks in the neighbourhood of Falkenham, yet he was always glad to come home to the little cottage, have a refreshing cup of tea, read the paper in the evening, nurse Mrs. Chapman's favourite cat on his knee, and sympathise with Chapman and his wife in their troubles. For even a farm labourer has his aspirations, his difficulties, his affections, his hopes, his disappointments, and his troubles like other more favourably-conditioned people.

Like most farm labouring couples, Chapman and his wife had had a large family. But, somehow or other, whether they lacked the care which more prosperous parents could have given them, or whether there was any hereditary weakness which had descended from grandparents or great-grandparents (Chapman and his wife were both strong and healthy), the children had all died when they were little, except one. This was the youngest, a girl, Althea, and you may be quite certain that she was a veritable "apple of the eye" to both father and mother.

The girl grew up, and like most girls took to "walking out" with a young man, a neighbour (evidently a most respectable and eligible young man) a porter at Trimley Station.

Althea and the young man were married, a favourable offer was subsequently made to him, and the upshot was that they emigrated to New South Wales.

This was the one great trouble of the worthy couple, the one great disappointment of their life. They did not wish to stand in the way of their daughter's advancement, but they could hardly bear the wrench which was necessary in order to part with their only surviving child. She and her husband were happy in their new home, yet Althea was the tender spot in the heart of both mother and father, and her name was never mentioned but tears came into their eyes.

They had dreamed rather than hoped that one day they might emigrate and be near her. But they were both getting old, and it could not be very long before they would be past arduous work, and there is no room for old used-up emigrants in the colonies.

"But why 'Althea'?" said Marmaduke one day to the father.

"Well, you see, sir, all our other children had been christened plain names, like John, William, or Mary. When they died, one after t'other, mother she goes to neighbour Johnson. Now neighbour Johnson she's a bit superstitious. 'Look you here, Mrs. Chapman,' she say to mother, 'do you name the next baby a grand book name out of a novel, and you see if that don't turn the luck. I've got an old novel what belonged to poor father, and he had a rare schooling; do you send me word the very minute the child's born, and

I'll look in the book, and the first name that catches my eye I'll tell you.' We did as she said, sir; and, sure enough, the first name she lighted on was 'Althea.'"

The baby was certainly lucky, for with such a system of chances, the poor infant might have been permanently endowed with a much less euphonious name than Althea.

Marmaduke had always been accustomed to shave; but since the railway disaster he had let his hair grow. So that by this time there were indications of a fairly good beard and whiskers, in addition to the moustachios which he had always been accustomed to wear. This had already altered his appearance to such an extent that, whether he ultimately intended to make himself known or not, he was perfectly certain, in his present condition, to remain unrecognised wherever he might go.

But the time was passing, and he felt that he ought to come to a decision one way or the other—either to go straight to London, announce his existence, and explain the mistake which had been made; or drift with events and allow people to imagine he was dead. But for several reasons he felt a strong inclination for the present to let things slide, watch the course of events, and see if there were a real indication of political events moving smoother now he was supposed to be dead. He therefore postponed his decision for a time.

CHAPTER XXV.

MARMADUKE FINDS THAT HE IS COMPELLED TO BE DEAD TO THE WORLD; HE THEREFORE DECIDES HENCEFORTH TO BE KNOWN AS ARTHUR HAMILTON.

MARMADUKE'S recovery was exceedingly slow.

Weeks grew into months.

Sometimes he thought that he should never wholly regain his normal health and strength.

He experienced at times peculiar sensations in his head. One moment his brain would be perfectly clear; the next moment he would be seized with a mental haziness, a partial forgetfulness, an inability to grasp effectively the particular idea which at that moment happened to be floating through his brain. This was probably an after-effect of the blow, accentuated by the work and worry to which he had been previously subjected.

The desire grew upon him to resume his active political work. But he knew that it would be madness to do this while his brain remained in a weak or injured condition.

Meanwhile the prognostications mentioned by *The Times* were certainly being fulfilled in a manner as rapid as remarkable. Marmaduke was supposed to be dead, but his star was still in the ascendant. It seemed as if his influence were growing and extending, even after that influence had been severed from the parent stem by death.

Marmaduke read and re-read *The Times* article. When he first read, " death, in his case has probably made all the difference between the rejection and the adoption of his most cherished schemes," the words did not seem to affect him greatly ; he did not apprehend their full significance. But, like an acid which is powerful but extremely slow in its action, they had gradually burnt into his very soul. If his influence increased, and if he accomplished far more when he was dead to the world, then why live?

In some strange way his work seemed to be in process of rapid development without him. However much his personal inclination might prompt him to come forth and make himself known, ought he to do so at the risk of putting back the clock of progress? It was certainly humiliating to feel, not that the dropped threads of his work had been taken up by other hands, but that in his absence those threads were being woven into warp and woof more expeditiously and more advantageously than they would have been by him.

After all he felt he had a good deal of human nature in him, and it is needless to deny that ambition and pride, either latent or apparent, lurked in some of the inmost recesses of that human nature.

But the peculiar position in which he found himself, and the strange development of events, did much to crush pride and obliterate ambition.

Marmaduke could not help seeing that there was some very serious and powerful force at work. This force seemed to say to him, with an irresistible voice, "Stand on one side! Your part in the work is ended. You are no longer necessary. The human power is exhausted; it must now give place to a transcendently superior moral and spiritual power. Stand on one side!"

From every point of view, therefore—physical, mental, and moral—his duty seemed perfectly clear. He must still remain hidden, and watch events.

Meanwhile, during these weary months of Marmaduke's inactivity, the news of the great Peace Conference was very cheering. The difficulties which had beset its deliberations seemed to be vanishing one after another.

To begin with, Russia, previously an opponent, was now a friend. Marmaduke read, with absorbing interest, all the news connected with recent events in Russia.

Rudolf von Lebenheim had spoken truly when he said that Russia was standing on the brink of a precipice, and that religious and political persecution, autocratic government, and corrupt administration, must inevitably cause an explosion which would shatter existing institutions, and so completely change the aspect of Russia that the Northern Colossus, as we have known it, would exist no longer.

The Revolution came. We know how profoundly it affected Marmaduke on that eventful night. But, to the surprise of everyone, instead of a reign of terror, instead of the horrors of civil war, instead of the disorders, and bloodshed, and anarchy which we usually associate with revolution, the change was effected in a most peaceable, calm, and orderly manner. The nation must have been in preparation for self-government for a long time, for she exhibited none of those weaknesses, none of that absence of self-reliance, which we are so accustomed to associate with the newly emancipated slave.

Russia emancipated herself; formed a strong representative provisional government; liberated her subject races; organised a confederation of the component parts of her vast empire. All this was done, too, with an absence of friction and an unanimity of purpose which was simply marvellous. The explosion had certainly produced an upheaval, but that upheaval had liberated a rejuvenated Russia. The world stood astonished at the birth which had taken place.

To give one instance how thoroughly Russia determined to cleanse her Augean Stable, it may be mentioned that no sooner was the revolution an accomplished fact, than the heads of the new administration determined upon the proper and sufficient remuneration of all government officials, and struck a death-blow to that notorious system of open bribery and corruption which had so long prevailed. One of the first acts of the new Russian Government, was to appoint fresh representatives to the Peace Conference—representatives who were in thorough sympathy with the aims and ideals of emancipated Russia. The effect was soon seen. The Russian representatives were now the foremost in advocating peace, conciliation, arbitration, and disarmament. None were more eager in upholding the influence or supporting the suggestions of the dead Marmaduke. Russia was indeed making enormous and rapid strides.

It is therefore not surprising that Marmaduke eagerly scanned all news connected with the great conference or the action of Russia. In most of the reports which he read in the newspapers, he was almost certain to come across some reference to the two great points in which he was so intimately concerned : (*a*) The growing influence of Marmaduke, and (*b*) His death adduced as the reason for this.

As some considerable time had now passed since Marmaduke's supposed death, and the change of government in Russia, the Conference had deliberated many times, and the press were expecting that an official announcement regarding the progress made would shortly be announced.

It was a very fine afternoon. Marmaduke had been sauntering along some of the pretty lanes of Falkenham, pondering and meditating as to the decision he should come to and when it must be taken. He had returned from the Felixstowe road, and had stopped at the Trimley Board School to have a word with the schoolmaster, and listen to the chatter of the children as they trooped out of the school. Leaving the school and talking with some of the children as he went along, he had nearly reached the windmill when he saw the miller drive up and enter the gateway to the mill.

As Marmaduke passed the gate the miller turned round and called out: " Rare news, Mr. Hamilton. I've just come from Ipswich, and coming through Carr Street I see a crowd round *The East Anglian*, and a big placard in the winder—' 'Special Edition End of Peace Conference. Detailed Report.' So I buys a copy; you can read it if you like, sir. I know you like to hear all the news."

Marmaduke thanked the man, took the paper, leant against the low fence by the side of the gate and opened the paper.

He had not read many sentences before he knew that the time for taking the decisive step had come. Should he come forth, or remain as he was.

The report he read was not lengthy. But it stated that the conference had terminated for the present. A perfect agreement had been arrived at, and (subject to the confirmation and ratification of the various governments) the draft treaty had been signed by the representatives of all the signatories to the two alliances, as well as the representatives of England, Spain, Portugal, Norway, Sweden, Denmark, Holland, and Belgium.

This treaty was on the basis of the great European Constitution left by Marmaduke, and found by the Emperor in the escritoire of the Telephone Room in the palace at Potsdam.

This treaty provided for a European Bund or Confederation of Nations, for an international conciliation board to settle international disputes, for a court of appeal or arbitration in cases of necessity, for ultimate and gradual disarmament, as well as for many points of minor interest.

The full text of this important document would be published so soon as it had been confirmed by the respective governments.

The report then went on to state that undoubtedly Europe owed this priceless document in a certain measure to the valuable suggestions, irrepressible ardour, and striking personality of a living Marmaduke, but in a much greater degree to the enormously increased influence which had been so strangely exerted by a dead Marmaduke.

The report continued :

"Europe gives a sigh of relief. The great war tension has now become further and definitely relaxed. People begin to regard a permanent peace, not as they have hitherto done, in a wistful, eager, longing, or even hopeful manner, but as a glorious present certainty."

In Marmaduke duty and conscientiousness were developed to a remarkable degree. When once he was convinced that a certain line of action was right, nothing would cause him to swerve from that line. At last the logic of events had succeeded in thoroughly persuading him that he could ensure the prosperity of the cause he had so much at heart—the cause of humanity, of peace, of righteousness—by allowing the world to think he was dead.

* * * * * *

The rubicon was past, an impassable gulf was behind him, retreat was impossible. Marmaduke had decided to remain dead to the world.

* * * * * *

Now that the irrevocable step was taken, he experienced new and strange feelings. He began to be conscious of what was involved in the word "death." There was no feeling of pain. No sensation at all, in fact. But he began to be aware that the spiritual essence and the physical entity of what had been combined in the term "Marmaduke" were no longer identical. A mysterious parting had taken place.

The influence, the spirit, the most important part of Marmaduke, was intensely alive; it was animating the world in an increasingly active manner. Marmaduke was daily discussed in the newspapers. His name was on everyone's tongue. He was looked up to, esteemed, loved as he never had been before. His words were treasured, his suggestions invested with the seal of authority. The magic name of Marmaduke was still a name to conjure with.

But Marmaduke the man existed no more. He who lived in the little black cottage at Falkenham was not Marmaduke. He was simply Arthur Hamilton. The two personalities henceforth were quite distinct. In fact, Arthur Hamilton began to regard the Marmaduke he read so much about as somebody quite distinct and apart from himself.

But Arthur Hamilton had another, and if possible, a stranger experience. He felt, with a growing sense of oppression and dismay, that he was as impotent to alter or modify his actions in the past as a man who has actually died and whose shade has revisited the scenes of his earthly career.

This impotence begat a strange desire. He longed for the opportunity to alter, add to, or erase some of the various memoranda and suggestions he had left behind him. The more his helplessness became apparent to him, the more this craving increased.

A flood of suggestions surged through his brain— they were useless. Oh, the pity of it! He had certainly worked arduously and unceasingly for the cause of humanity, but the hardest work of all, for a man of his temperament, was to "rest and wait patiently."

Certainly, he, of all men, had no cause to reproach himself with wasted opportunities; but as idea after idea floated through his brain—ideas which he knew would never bear fruit—they seemed to take up a never ending and melancholy chorus: "too late, too late, too late!"

CHAPTER XXVI.

HOW ARTHUR HAMILTON BECOMES A REPORTER ON THE STAFF OF "THE EAST ANGLIAN DAILY TIMES."

SOME months have elapsed since the events recorded in the last chapter.

Arthur Hamilton still adheres to his resolution, and consequently still remains Arthur Hamilton.

Rest, enforced freedom from political worry, and the bracing air of Falkenham and its neighbourhood have done their work effectually. Arthur's health is completely renewed. He feels as strong, if not stronger than he ever did before; his brain is clear, and he possesses his normal energy.

He still lodges at Chapman's little cottage, and the renewed state of his health is in no small degree due to the assiduous care of the worthy couple. By a plausible tale he was soon able to allay their anxiety, as well as that of Dr. Smith, regarding his friends.

He has lately commenced a new life.

Before the cash with which he found himself possessed after the railway disaster was exhausted, he knew that he must go out into the world and earn his living. He found the world new and strange. He was unknown—obviously he could present no record, give no credentials. He soon found that he really stood in a worse position than he did when, a good many years before, he quitted studies and entered upon the career of a journalist.

Of course his first thought was that he could not do better than again enter that profession for which he was pre-eminently fitted. Accordingly, late one afternoon, he crossed the threshold of the handsome building in Carr Street, Ipswich, and asked to see the editor of *The East Anglian Daily Times*. The editor was in London. Arthur called again. He called thrice. At last his patience was rewarded. One day, after waiting some considerable time, he was ushered into the presence of the great man. He was a genial-looking, grey-haired man. Arthur introduced himself as an applicant for a post of reporter. He explained that for reasons which it was scarcely necessary to discuss, he was obliged to earn a living. He had received a liberal education, knew shorthand, could report verbatim, condense, rapidly transcribe, was a rapid typewriter, and flattered himself he was a good paragraphist, could write a racy leader, or send home descriptive articles as a special correspondent. Would the editor give him a trial?

The editor elevated his eyebrows. "Then you have doubtless had plenty of experience. What have you done? You doubtless have references. On what newspaper have you been employed? You can probably show me some examples of your work?"

Arthur was reluctantly obliged to confess he could produce neither one nor the other.

Whether the editor felt that such glowing qualifications were largely the result of the applicant's imagination, or whether he was suspicious that Arthur's antecedents were shady, is immaterial.

The grey-haired gentleman was polite, but frigid. " I regret to say that there is no vacancy on our staff at present, and we are obliged to refuse all outside copy. I will keep your name and address by me, and will let you know in case there is a vacancy. Good-day, Mr. Hamilton." And Arthur found himself bowed out of the editorial sanctum, without having received the slightest hope that he would be granted a trial, even in the humblest capacity, upon the staff of this important provincial daily paper.

Many men would have been disheartened at this rebuff. Some would have tried another mode of earning money. More would have carried their wares to another market.

But our friend, the editor of *The East Anglian Daily Times*, had not the slightest idea of the pertinacity, the indomitable energy, and the dogged perseverance of the gentleman with whom he had to deal.

The rebuff only put Arthur on his mettle. He did not do as some would have done who possessed his pertinacity—worry the editor by calling again and again, notwithstanding repeated rejections, and play the part of the importunate widow.

Arthur saw the difficulties connected with his peculiar position, in which he was powerless to produce either record or references. He opened a battery in quite another direction, and bombarded the obdurate editor with journalistic products.

If any social event of importance occurred, Arthur was on the spot, and sent a paragraph in his best style. He reported several meetings in Ipswich, transcribed his notes while the speakers were uttering sentences of an uninteresting character, sent in his notes there and then, and beat the official reporters in despatch and accuracy.

For a long time these reports and paragraphs were wasted. They were not even glanced at by the editor, but were thrown into the editorial wastepaper-basket unread. But Arthur never desisted. He soon became well known to the rival reporters. They laughed at him, and called him the "reporting crank." Then they were irritated by his pertinacity and became jealous. Neither ridicule nor jealousy was of any avail. Arthur gradually overcame their raillery by his imperturbable manner, and vanquished their jealousy by helping them and giving them hints. They could not withstand his good nature, and they soon recognised his superior ability. One of them, who was about to leave Ipswich for a higher position on the staff of a Midland daily paper, spoke so well of him to the chief at Carr Street, that the grey-headed editor at length sent for him, and gave him a subordinate position at a low salary. This quite satisfied Arthur. He knew that the thin end once inserted, he would not have much difficulty in driving the wedge home. In the meantime two points were gained. He was saved from actual want, and he was enabled to ensure payment on a fairly liberal scale to his humble host and hostess.

For, with the generosity and delicate feeling frequently possessed by the poor, they had resolutely, or, as Arthur told them, obstinately, refused to be reimbursed anything beyond their actual out-of-pocket expenses in connection with his illness and board. His whole bearing told them without any words from him that he was in some kind of distress—they knew not what or how, and they were determined not to make a market of him. But now that he was earning money he was able to prevail upon them to accept a weekly sum a little in advance of what he cost them.

Although he was now permanently attached to the staff of the *East Anglian Daily Times* and growing in favour, both with the chief and with his fellow reporters, he still made the little cottage at Falkenham his headquarters.

It is needless to say that the elderly couple were very much attached to him. For, true to his nature, he could not help loving and sympathising with his labourer host and hostess. He was their guide, philosopher, and friend.

Their living room was sufficiently large to be comfortable, and sufficiently small to be cosy.

Nearly the whole of one side of the room was occupied by a huge open fireplace, containing two real old-fashioned chimney corner seats, now almost obsolete. Round this large opening were oak jambs, head and shelf, forming a simple but exquisitely moulded chimney piece. There were no enrichments such as may be seen in some of the few remaining ancient buildings in Ipswich, but the mouldings were delicate and bore the stamp of refinement. The chimney piece was evidently very old, and was just one which would rejoice the heart of an archæologist or architect.

Occupying one side of the spacious fireplace in this really comfortable cottage sitting-room, was a large bread baking oven, and in the adjoining kitchen or scullery were the usual appliances for brewing. For the humblest labouring household in the district would have considered itself covered with indelible disgrace if it could not, or at any rate did not, do its own baking and brewing.

Nothing delighted Arthur so much as to have the opportunity in his spare time, which of course generally happened in the morning and afternoon, to help the husband with his brewing or the wife with her baking. Arthur, moreover, was by no means to be despised as a gardener. Both Chapman and his wife were wont to declare that the garden at the back of their little cottage had never looked so tidy, nor had borne so much produce, as since Mr. Hamilton had been with them.

John Chapman, after all, was only a labourer. He was accustomed to receive from those with whom he came in contact just that treatment, neither more nor less, which is usually accorded to a labourer. As a labourer, he was naturally unaccustomed to those subtle refinements of manner which characterise educated people. When, therefore, he and his good wife were brought into daily intercourse with such a sympathetic, refined, educated gentleman as Arthur Hamilton—for Arthur was essentially a gentle man—can we wonder that there gradually grew in both of them an intense love and affection for him? For Arthur treated Chapman as one gentleman should treat another, and was as deferential, polite, and agreeable to Mrs. Chapman as if she had been a titled lady. It had always been part of Arthur's nature to honour womanhood, whether in the guise of a princess or of a farm labourer's wife.

Arthur was very fond of children, and for a considerable radius from the little cottage he was certain to have small companions of both sexes, who would put their chubby, sometimes dirty, hands in his, or hang on to his coat, whenever he took his walks abroad and they were within sight. They very soon found out that he was sympathetic, and immediately became correspondingly confidential. In fact, Arthur's latent sense of chivalry was always aroused whenever he found himself in the presence of either weakness or suffering. To give an instance. In the village of Falkenham there lived, or rather existed, a half-demented, helpless, harmless epileptic boy of fourteen, who was better known by his nickname of Silly Billy than by his proper name of William Hart. Before Arthur's advent this poor lad was tormented by all the small children of the neighbourhood, as well as by many who were old enough and big enough to know better. So helpless was this afflicted boy, that he seemed powerless to oppose the stones thrown at him by babies who could only just toddle.

When Arthur came, he kindly but firmly put a stop to all this. The children soon came to be aware that they would lose Mr. Hamilton's friendship if they teased Silly Billy. And Mr. Hamilton's friendship was so precious a boon, that the loss of it was too terrible a contingency for the minds of the Falkenham children to contemplate.

So much, therefore, did Arthur's sympathetic nature influence the children, that the current of their actions became completely turned; kindness took the place of stones and mud, and poor Silly Billy began to think, as well as the confusion in his head would let him, that the world was a much pleasanter one now than it ever had been before.

So Arthur's life sped on. Take it all in all, he was certainly happy. It is true that he lodged in a labourer's cottage, and earned just a little more than was sufficient to supply his actual physical wants.

But his work was congenial, his responsibilities were *nil*, he was in daily contact with loving sympathetic people, and he was conscious that the great work to which he had devoted himself body and soul, was being rapidy carried forward.

One day, in the course of his journalistic duties, he read a paragraph which gave him a thrill: a peculiar thrill. It gave him a nervous cold chill, as if a whiff of air from a freshly-opened grave had blown across him. It caused Arthur to strike his forehead with the palm of his hand, and ejaculate " Am I then really dead ? "

The paragraph was as follows:

"As we recently intimated, the Dean of Westminster has now caused a tablet to the memory of Marmaduke to be placed in one of the vacant spaces in the Abbey. The inscription is simple but touching: 'Sacred to the memory of Marmaduke, who was instrumental in freeing Europe from the thraldom of militarism, in abolishing war, in averting a social revolution, and in lifting the burdens from millions of weary shoulders.'

"In unveiling the tablet the Dean said a few touching and pathetic words, and concluded:

"'Marmaduke was a born reformer. The spirit of true progress animated every fibre of his being. Without, perhaps, being aware of it, he was consecrated heart and soul to the benefit of humanity. It is inexpressibly sad that orthodoxy, whether of religion or politics, so frequently ignored when it did not actually oppose him. It was the old story—genius *versus* orthodoxy—and in the long run genius won, as it always has won, and always will win.

"'How to make the daily life of the people happier, better, higher, nobler, was a problem always in his thoughts. He returned to this theme again and again, as Chopin went back again and again to the theme of music which touched his soul. May the reverberations of that theme continue to be heard throughout the coming ages, and may it never be said that the influence of Marmaduke, like his physical life, has ceased to exist."

A week or two after this he read another paragraph, which caused a thrill of a totally different nature. This time the blood went coursing through his veins with unwonted vigour and a hot flush was diffused over his whole frame. At first he experienced a feeling of glad pleasure, but this soon gave way to sharp stabs of pain. He began to realise the peculiarly painful pleasure which lies hidden in the fact that it is "better to have loved and lost than never to have loved at all."

The paragraph was as follows:

"It has recently leaked out that at an early period in the career of Marmaduke some love passages, which were on the eve of terminating in an engagement, passed between him and Fraulein von Lebenheim, sister to the well-known Rudolf von Lebenheim of the German diplomatic service.

"These love passages ultimately came to nothing, but it is an open secret that the lady mourns for the dead Marmaduke as for a first and only love.

"Upon being made acquainted with this fact, the Emperor, who takes a keen interest in anyone and everyone who has at any time had personal relationship with his much loved late illustrious coadjutor, has offered to honour the lady in question by raising her to the dignity of a countess in her own right."

CHAPTER XXVII.

GIVES A RAPID GLANCE AT THE PROGRESS OF EVENTS, AND TELLS HOW IT IS PROPOSED TO APPOINT A DAY COMMEMORATIVE OF THE LIFE AND WORKS OF MARMADUKE.

TIME passed on. Arthur Hamilton worked hard and conscientiously, and rapidly gained the confidence of the grey-haired chief.

Of course the greater portion of Arthur's time was necessarily spent in the vicinity of his work; therefore he found it convenient to obtain lodgings in the neighbourhood of Ipswich. But he still made Chapman's house his headquarters. He looked upon the little cottage as home, and spent at Falkenham the spare time which remained at his disposal.

Meantime many events occurred in the political world.

After Marmaduke's supposed tragic end, and upon the reassembling of the conference, the German Emperor was again proposed and unanimously elected Honorary President of the Conference.

But more honours were in store for the Emperor.

All the various principalities and dependencies which go to make up the great German Empire recognised how much they owed to their Kaiser for his courage and energetic action in promoting and developing the new order; in causing his country to take the leading position in European policy ; and in stamping himself as the foremost monarch-champion of righteousness and peace.

In gratitude and love, therefore, the Federal Council and the Reichstag passed a measure by which the title of Emperor of Germany was substituted for that of German Emperor.

But the star of the German Emperor was still further in the ascendant.

For when the members of the conference had finished their deliberations, presented their report, and the conference, as a conference, existed no longer, the Emperor of Germany was approached by the associated governments and requested to become the chairman of the proposed European Bund.

Gradual and uniform disarmament was already being carried out. The ratepayers of all countries (especially the continental military nations subject to conscription) were beginning to experience the benefit of peace. Trade and commerce and the peaceful arts were developing by leaps and bounds.

The name of Marmaduke was everywhere mentioned and everywhere received with marks of greater love and greater enthusiasm than ever. The influence of Marmaduke was still increasing.

But it was not only the tax-payers who discovered that they were receiving benefits from the new order.

One of the first edicts of the European Bund consisted of a declaration of absolute religious equality and liberty of conscience to all subjects of the sovereignties and confederacies within its jurisdiction.

No longer was an Orthodox Greek Church able to persecute a Stundist. By this international decree religions were recognised as moral and spiritual forces only, Churches were severed from State control, and were deprived of all exclusive power and privileges. All religious communities and sects were, *cæteris paribus*, so far as the State was concerned, on an equality. The question of endowments was in all cases left to be determined by the Parliament of each particular State.

And so died by a natural death, with scarcely a struggle or convulsion, the principle of the State establishment of religion.

Thus it came to pass that the Church of England found itself disestablished by a force which it was powerless to arrest, and those who were advocating the liberation of religion from State control found their aims accomplished without the necessity for that prolonged parliamentary and religious struggle which they had anticipated. Religious persecution of every shade came to an end at the same moment that all countries embraced in the Bund were thrown open to religious teachers or missionaries of any religion or sect.

Another decree promulgated by the Bund related to universal suffrage and representative government. Whilst kings and sovereigns, where they existed, were not deprived of one iota of their dignity, autocracy was doomed. The Bund was determined to carry out the grand ideal of "government of the people for the people by the people."

From the moment this principle was adopted, hereditary legislators and other similar anomalies were of course doomed. That which could not have been abolished in England except at the risk of a serious revolution, ceased to exist upon the edict of the Bund. Consequently the English House of Lords as at present constituted, magistrates appointed as the nominees of a political party, and aldermen who had never been before the electorate, became impossible.

Under the new *régime*, weak points in administration and anomalies in government soon discovered themselves. At the earliest moment the Bund strengthened the former, and rectified the latter.

For instance—in Republican France, which boasted of its representative institutions, an autocratic sovereign had continued to exist in the person of the Prefect of Police. This official represented a sovereign arbitrary power; he was the political servant of whatever power happened to be at the head of affairs—Emperor, King, or Republican Ministers. The Prefect of Police, in fact, was practically entitled to act with perfect despotism. The Bund changed all this, and placed him in his proper position—the servant of the people instead of its master.

Arthur Hamilton was in excellent spirits. He seldom read the political news without rejoicing. For with each decree issued by the Bund, and with every action taken under that decree, the influence of Marmaduke increased. The associated governments seemed saturated through and through with those grand ideals of righteousness which became crystallised in the minds of the common people under the comprehensive term "Marmaduke."

One day Arthur read, with mingled feelings, the following announcement in *The Times*:

"Upon the initiative of the Emperor of Germany, the European Bund has arranged to

17

appoint a day commemorative of the life and works of the still mighty Marmaduke. The exact date has not yet been determined. Upon that day all public offices will be closed, and there will practically be a public holiday throughout the European States embraced in the Bund. But each State will have a perfectly free hand as to the manner in which the commemoration day will be kept. The official recognition will consist of a religious service in which the Sovereigns and Presidents as well as the chief Statesmen and leading representative men of the associated States will take part. As Marmaduke was an Englishman, and the Great Peace Conference was held and brought to a successful termination in London, it has been thought fitting that this religious service should be held in Westminster Abbey. It is needless to say that this service will be most solemn and impressive. We have reason to believe that features will be introduced into this service which will render it absolutely unique in the history of Europe. It is certain that those who have the great privilege to be present will witness one of the most magnificent religious services ever held."

*　　*　　*　　*　　*　　*

The day was fixed, a detailed programme of the proceedings was published, and the whole world was talking of the Commemoration Day, and how it was to be observed in each State and each locality. In some cases money was to be collected to erect and endow philanthropic institutions. In some cases the poor were to receive especial consideration. In other cases the children were thought of. But chief interest centred in the wonderful service which was to be held in Westminster Abbey. Naturally applications for tickets were received in overwhelming numbers. The selection of the favoured few was most difficult. Elaborate measures were devised by temporary galleries for increasing the seating accommodation of the Abbey to its utmost limit. Every inch of possible space was utilised. But even then the applications received exceeded a hundred times the seats at the disposal of the authorities.

True, however, to its democratic tendencies, the Bund, after providing a limited number of seats for royal personages and leading and representative men of each country, and the press, determined to allot the whole of the remainder to the general public.

To prevent confusion, crushing, and waiting for hours outside the doors, all these public seats were to be allotted by ballot. Those who wished to obtain a seat were to send in a written application. The name of the applicant was registered in a book and marked with a number. Upon a certain day a ballot was taken, and the name of the lucky person affixed to each winning number received a ticket to a numbered and reserved seat.

One day the chief called Arthur into the editorial room, and offered him a ticket for the press gallery—a much coveted honour—and asked him to supply a descriptive account of the proceedings in the Abbey.

To the chief's great astonishment Arthur begged to be excused. For he knew that, with his high strung nervous organisation, the ordeal of simply being present would be almost too much for him. To carry out any journalistic duty under such circumstances would be altogether out of the question. Still Arthur longed to be present. He felt that, cost what it might, he must look once more, perhaps for the last time, upon the face of his revered friend, the Emperor of Germany, and once more glance at the other familiar faces of those who would take part in this memorable service.

Neither Arthur's presence nor his absence could now have the slightest effect upon humanity, beneficially or otherwise—the rule by which he had always gauged his actions. So he determined to leave to chance the decision in the matter. He would make application for an admission ticket in the ordinary way, as one of the general public. If, as he anticipated, he were unsuccessful, he would rest content. If, on the other hand, his number proved to be a winning one, he would accept the situation and be present.

In the meantime he made a considerable effort to dismiss the matter from his mind, and proceed with his journalistic duties as if no memorial service were about to take place.

Time passed on, when one morning, much to his surprise, he received through the post an intimation that he had been allotted a reserved seat. He was one of the favoured few upon whom the ballot box had smiled. In due course he received an elaborately printed and decorated admission ticket, a triumph of the colour-printer's art.

The chief was astounded when he heard the news. He could scarcely believe that any rising journalist who had his way to make, much less his favourite

Arthur, could be so idiotic as to throw away a chance, which might never occur again, to do a brilliant stroke of descriptive reporting, upon such a historic occasion as the memorial service to the great Marmaduke ; and quietly sit amongst the audience.

Such a foolish proceeding was quite beyond the comprehension of the grey-haired editor.

The evening before the eventful Commemoration Day arrived. Honest John Chapman and his worthy wife were much exercised regarding their whilom lodger, now friend, Arthur Hamilton.

" He do seem that bad at times lately that he fare as if he was going to be real ill again," said the former to the latter as they sat late on this particular evening in their cosy little living room. " I don't like the look of him at all, mother."

" No more do I, John," responded the wife. " And I'm sure he's not fit to go up to-morrow to that wonderful affair at the Abbey. Such a lot of grand doings and excitement 'll be too much for his nerves, I know it will. I tried to get him off going, but it was no good. He's bent on being there."

And, foolish and absurd as it may seem, the worthy couple actually then and there concocted a plot, by which the husband should, unknown to his lodger, go up by an early train to town the next morning, proceed to the vicinity of the Abbey, and endeavour to keep Arthur in sight as he entered and left the building. In fact, play the part of the unseen, hovering angel.

CHAPTER XXVIII.

THE DAY OF COMMEMORATION—WESTMINSTER ABBEY—THE CROWD AND THE PROCESSION.

THE morning of the great day of Commemoration arrived. Excitement in London was intense. Barriers had been erected near all the entrances to the Abbey to prevent crushing and to allow ticket holders to enter in comfort. Upon all the available open spaces along the route which the procession of royalties and others who attended the proceedings was to take, huge galleries of seats had been erected. The crowds along the whole of this route, and especially in the vicinity of the Abbey, were enormous. Flags fluttered from a thousand windows and gates and roofs and other points. The day was magnificent; the sky was cloudless; and there seemed a buoyancy in the air which exhilarated everyone.

There was undoubtedly a spirit of rejoicing abroad which was infectious. From the hearts of the people a deep feeling of thankfulness and joy spontaneously welled up and overflowed. Every sign of popular enthusiasm and popular joy was visible. And yet the ostensible object of the great gathering, the solemn service, the vast crowds, was to commemorate the works and life of a man who was dead! Then why the rejoicing, why the thankfulness? Strange to say, the death of the man was swallowed up, absolutely lost sight of, in the great work he had accomplished and the increasing influence which his name and his memory exerted.

Ask the first intelligent-looking man in the crowd why he was there and why he rejoiced? You would find that he would make no reference to the death of Marmaduke, but would tell you that he was there and he was rejoicing because to him "Marmaduke" was a word which signified a policy of justice, peace, and happiness, such as the world had never known before. And this man in the crowd would probably conclude his reference to Marmaduke by exclaiming "Long may he live." In point of fact, strange as it may seem, the life, the true life, of this remarkable man had so overcome his death, that several times during the day, more especially when the grand procession was passing, hundreds of people were so carried away by their excited enthusiasm that they shouted "Long live Marmaduke." And this singular cry of "Long live Marmaduke" was taken up and echoed and re-echoed from point to point along the route.

In the history of London, nay, in the history of the world, never before had such crowds gathered under such circumstances to pay such homage to such a man.

But the homage did not end with the masses. So far as the procession itself was concerned, more magnificent and spectacular pageants had doubtless been witnessed many times. There were no brilliant uniforms, no blare of military bands, no calvacade of soldiers, no shimmer of unsheathed swords, no glint of steel cuirasses, no flutter of pennoned lances, no kaleidoscopic combinations of colour which are usually associated with a procession of sovereigns. This procession might have been voted very tame by the mere sightseer. Bnt the sight was rendered infinitely more impressive, infinitely more thrilling, by reason of its very simplicity. For such a gathering and such a procession of associated sovereigns, statesmen, leaders, and representatives, all occupied in doing honour to a man, his life, his influence, and his principles, were absolutely unique in the world's history.

With the sole exception of the associated sovereigns, who wore their uniforms for a reason which will be afterwards apparent, the costumes and the dresses were plain and simple. In the procession, all these sovereigns, whether emperors, kings, or queens, as well as the presidents of the republics embraced in the Bund, were all on an absolute equality.

The procession started from Buckingham Palace, skirted the Green Park to Hyde Park Corner, passed along Piccadilly, the southern end of Regent Street, a portion of Waterloo Place, Cockspur Street, and so reached Trafalgar Square. Thence along Whitehall through Parliament Street, past the Houses of Parliament, until it reached the Abbey, where the distinguished persons passed direct into the Chapter House, there to be received by the high dignitaries of the Abbey.

First come the minor officials, then the representative and leading men in arts and science in each country, then the statesmen and political leaders, and finally the associated titular heads of the various empires, kingdoms, and republics embraced in the great European Bund.

The place of honour was naturally given to the venerable and beloved Empress-Queen—who had long passed the allotted term of years, but who still enjoyed a hale, green old age—supported by him to whom for some years past had been delegated the task of wielding the sceptre of active sovereignty, the ever popular Edward VII.

The crowd did not of course recognise all the occupants of the carriages in this long and unique procession, but there was scarcely one of the hundreds of personages composing it, whose name was not a familiar household word to the newspaper readers of all countries.

For the first time in the history of royal pageants, the task of escorting the procession and guarding the route was not monopolised by the military forces.

The ceremony was so essentially a religious and civil one, intended to commemorate the advent of peace and the overthrow in Europe of militarism, that it would have been scarcely fitting that military escorts and guards should be prominent.

In point of fact, although ample means were taken by the civil authorities for regulating the traffic, keeping the crowds within their proper bounds, and protecting the persons of London's guests from the possible vagaries of madmen, of escorts and guards as hitherto understood there were none.

But we must return to our friend Chapman. The kind-hearted labourer had actually carried out his ridiculous idea. He had come up to London by the very earliest train on this memorable morning, and had made his way straight to the Abbey with a dogged determination of taking up a position as near the western door as possible; for he knew that it was at this door that Arthur's ticket was available. Chapman had told his wife he thought there might be a "goodish crowd," and that he might have to stand in the same spot several hours. But he was scarcely prepared for the sight which he saw. When he arrived, he found to his dismay that hundreds of people had already come, and he saw no prospect of being able to stand within a reasonable distance of even the opening in the external barrier through which his friend would have to pass. But Chapman was used to roughing it, and was not afraid of a few hard knocks. By dint of squeezing an inch here and an inch there, of perseverance, and of taking advantage of every movement of those in front of him, he at last succeeded in gradually wedging himself until he came within ten or a dozen feet of the much coveted position. Despite his utmost efforts he could advance no farther. He was so squeezed, however, by the people in front of him, behind him, and on each side of him, that he felt he was perfectly powerless to go to the rescue of his friend even if that friend had needed his assistance ever so greatly.

The privileged and fortunate ticket-holders commenced to arrive. Then they came in greater numbers. Poor Chapman used his utmost exertions to endeavour to catch a sight of the arrivals, but his bent form materially reduced a stature which under most favourable circumstances was not above the medium height. Consequently, so far as seeing anything or anybody was concerned, he might as well have been at Falkenham in his little cottage. Arthur Hamilton duly arrived, passed within a few feet of his friend, but of course neither saw nor was seen by Chapman.

When all the ticket-holders had arrived, the procession had passed, and the service in the Abbey had commenced, a movement took place in the crowd. Many were tired of standing so long and went away. Many considered they had seen all that there was to be seen at the west door, and tried to get nearer to the north door so that they might have a chance of seeing the Royal personages as they emerged after the service.

Chapman found therefore, to his great joy, that very soon after the service commenced, the crowd in front of him began to melt away, and he could easily take up a position close to the opening in the barrier which led to the west door.

"I don't mind," he said to himself. "If I didn't see Mr. Hamilton go in, I shall be certain to see him come out ; and perhaps, after all, it's just as well he didn't see me when he went in."

CHAPTER XXIX.

INSIDE WESTMINSTER ABBEY. AN IMPRESSIVE CEREMONY. A STARTLING PROCLAMATION. A MENTAL TRAGEDY, AND AN UNEXPECTED VISION.

THE arrangements for the ceremony had been carefully prepared and published beforehand. Each portion of the proceedings had not only been set forth, but accurately timed; so that everyone both inside and outside the Abbey knew exactly what would take place, and the moment of its occurrence.

Let us follow Arthur Hamilton, as he entered the Abbey. He was early, and when he first took his seat many of the privileged spectators had not arrived.

The seats gradually filled up, until all were occupied. The sight was then grand. Not a spare space was unoccupied. No matter where one directed one's gaze, it met a sea of faces and heads. A strange solemnity pervaded the vast assembly. All had their programmes. All knew what was coming, yet, strange to say, a state of high tension prevailed.

An indescribable excitement was none the less apparent because it was subdued and suppressed. For it was felt that there was more in this commemorative ceremony than met the eye or the general understanding.

As Arthur looked round he experienced a singular emotion. He thought it must be a dream. He could hardly convince himself that he was awake. After all, was he not the actuating motive in the drama about to be enacted ? Was he not the centre and the focus of this wonderful demonstration ? And yet he sat there unrecognised and alone ! It must be a dream.

A few minutes before the time arrived for the service to commence, an opening voluntary was played on the organ. Solemn and impressive, the tones of the organ reverberated through the building, and then died away in a deep diapason, which was felt rather than heard. Then the grand instrument throbbed and trembled, as if it were conscious that it was taking part in an awe-inspiring ceremony.

Suddenly the opening note of a processional hymn was heard. Immediately the vast assembly rose. It was the signal that the distinguished visitors, who had previously been received by the authorities of the Abbey in the Chapter House, were being conducted to the seats allotted to them in a prominent position on each side of the steps leading to the altar.

First came a procession consisting of choir, clergy, and high dignitaries of the church. Mingled with the latter, and on a footing of equality— a graceful act on the part of the episcopal authorities, and an act befitting the occasion—were seen prominent representatives of other religious bodies. As a matter of fact, they were still called nonconformists, but since the principle of religious equality had been universally adopted, "nonconformity" and "nonconformists" were words which of course had entirely lost their original meaning.

Following the religious leaders, came the guests of the occasion, the titular heads of the associated governments; the sovereigns and presidents. It was then observed for the first time that they were all clad in white mantles, which hung in graceful folds from shoulders to feet, cloaks which covered, but did not conceal, the brilliant military uniforms worn by most of the sovereigns. Material and trimming of these mantles were white, spotless white, with the exception of a conspicuous blood-red cross worked upon the left breast. It was an unmistakable token that Christianity and peace had finally eclipsed militarism and war in Europe. Here were veritable knights of a new order of Rosicrucians; a new order of crusaders.

But who is this bowed female figure to whom is accorded the especial honour of walking amongst the crowned heads of Europe?—a figure vividly conspicuous by being attired in deep mourning; for, by general consent, mourning had been universally discarded on this great day of rejoicing and commemoration.

Arthur was abruptly brought back from dreamland to the world of reality, for with throbbing heart and thrilling nerves, he instantly recognised in the bowed, mourning figure, Alicia, Countess Lebenheim.

Their paths had not crossed since that eventful day when, from a stern sense of duty, they had mutually rejected one another. A crowd of thoughts chased one another through Arthur's brain at the unexpected sight of Alicia. What might have been—what was.

The wound in his heart which love had made, the wound which he imagined had permanently healed, but which after all had only superficially closed, was torn open and began to bleed. It was not to be wondered, that, in Arthur's eyes, Alicia was an abnormally prominent figure in the unique ceremony which followed.

Arthur had his programme on his knee, but he never consulted it.

He was certainly conscious that a very simple and impressive service was held. He knew that the whole of the immense multitude stood up and sang "All people that on earth do dwell" to the "Old Hundredth" tune. He knew that 1 Corinthians xiii. (revised version), was read as a lesson by the chairman of the Congregational Union. He knew that a number of prayers, specially composed by the Primate, were recited. He knew that a sympathetic address was delivered by the learned and popular Dean of Westminster, and that the theme of this address was "the universal reign of the Divine Prince of Peace." He heard, with a feeling of familiarity, the anthem and chorale composed by himself. He heard the Magnificat and Nunc Dimittis sung to special settings. He stood up when the congregation stood up, and sat down when they sat down. He was outwardly attentive. But his thoughts were not with the service.

Marmaduke's chorale on the grand old hymn—

> It came upon the midnight clear,
>   That glorious song of old,
> From angels bending near the earth
>   To touch their harps of gold ;
> ' Peace on the earth, goodwill to men,
>   From heaven's all-gracious King';
> The world in solemn stillness lay
>   To hear the angels sing—

was sung by the entire congregation, and created a profound impression. The melody was simple, it was in unison, and by this time had become well-known to the public.

As verse succeeded verse the vast congregation caught the spirit of the hymn.

Whilst they sang—

> Look up, for lo ! the peaceful years
>   Come swiftly on the wing,

they recognised that the peaceful years had already arrived, the age of gold had come !

So from congregation, as well as from choir, burst forth such a volume of joyful song as had never before been heard in the old Abbey ; a song all the more joyful because it expressed neither an aspiration, nor a hope, nor an ideal, but a glorious fulfilment.

The concluding words of the last verse were scarcely ended, when everyone prepared to witness the most important part of the ceremony.

The associated sovereigns and presidents, led by the Emperor of Germany, filed out of their seats, advanced to the foot of the altar and then turned and faced the huge assembly.

The Kaiser was about to speak. The nervous

tension of the expectant congregation increased. The stillness was most profound. What would the Emperor have to say regarding his dead friend Marmaduke? In any case everyone felt that an epoch-making speech would be delivered. The vast audience almost held its breath when the Emperor commenced to speak.

Now Arthur experienced another emotion.

As a rapid panorama of his past life is said to pass with lightning speed through the brain of a drowning man, so flashed across Arthur's memory that past of social and political reform with which the Kaiser and he had been so intimately associated. He was again in dreamland.

It is frequently recorded that at an important crisis in a man's life, what we are pleased to regard and designate as trivial things, will force themselves with undue prominence upon his vision and his attention.

So with Arthur. At the time when one would have imagined that he could not possibly have been distracted by such a trifle, he was closely watching a bright ray of sunlight which gleamed through a south window, and lost itself in the space between the arches opposite.

Arthur was closely watching the ray of light when the Emperor spoke. The illustrious monarch's words were simple and most impressive.

Commencing with the personal aspect of the question he pronounced an affectionate eulogy upon his dead friend.

But the eulogy seemed merely to refer to some far and away stranger, so absorbed was the brain of

Arthur in the contemplation of that wonderful panorama; and so closely did the eyes of Arthur follow that moving ray of light.

The Emperor continued: "We are assembled here to commemorate by a solemn service the works of a great man.

"If we were merely thinking of a great man's death, we might deplore that the indomitable energy, the grand achievement, the wonderful personality, were things of the past.

"It is true that Marmaduke, the man, has died. But he has shown us how truly the entrance to life is through death. He has already risen from the dead with infinitely multiplied vitality. His spirit is abroad to-day, here and everywhere, influencing thoughts and animating actions.

"At the present moment, Marmaduke is the most vital force with which we have to deal.

"That is why we declare this Marmaduke is not dead, but living. Now, it being conceded beyond the shadow of a doubt that Marmaduke is the most potent force in Europe, it is only fitting that we recognise that force in a manner which is unmistakable. It is, therefore, the desire of my co-rulers in the European Bund, that the practical creator of that Bund shall be accorded that rank and title which are his by right."

At this point the Emperor and his military colleagues drew their swords and raised them above their heads. Those rulers who had not swords simply raised their right hands. Then rang through the building the startling words:

"We proclaim Marmaduke, Emperor of Europe!"

The moment these words were uttered Arthur experienced another emotion; this time severe and crushing.

He saw himself an Emperor and yet unknown; a mighty conqueror and yet unrecognised; the cynosure of all eyes and yet unseen.

He saw the adamantine nature of the barrier which fate had erected between himself and the grandest position the world had ever seen. Should he acknowledge his impotence and yield to fate. Or should he dash against that barrier and break through it or perish?

* * * * * *

The ray of light still moved forward.

Arthur trembled with the fierce emotion. But this emotion was not seen by those sitting on each side of him. They were not aware of the awful mental tragedy being enacted so close to them.

The thought of silence was maddening to Arthur.

"If I remain silent," he pondered, "what do I incur? A living death! Horrible! If I remain silent I live, but the cerements of the grave will always cling round me. I am dead! Dead to participation in further progress. Dead to participation in the glorious future which I see before me. The glory is actually before me. But it is slipping, slipping, slipping away. I must grasp it. I feel I am being suffocated—suffocated in my mind, suffocated in my soul, with a suffocation worse, far worse than physical suffocation. I cannot endure it. A word will set me free. I must utter the cry, 'Marmaduke is not dead, he is alive; I am Marmaduke!'

"Oh, the irony of fate! The Emperor, my one devoted friend, is selected to pronounce my death sentence. If he only knew! If he only knew!

"Oh, the irony of fate! I am alone, alone! Not a word of sympathy is possible for me!"

"My eyes are opened. I now know that I had ambition, frightful ambition. I imagined I was solely actuated by a love for humanity. Oh, vain imagining! I now know that in my heart of hearts I aspired to be crowned such an earthly emperor as they are now proclaiming me. The cup of my ambition is truly filled to overflowing. It is held before me. I must drink it. I cannot let it pass by me. I must speak or die!"

* * * * * *

The ray of light still moved forward.

The Kaiser continued:

"Had Marmaduke been now living in the flesh, such a ceremony as this, such a proclamation as this, would have been impossible.

"But in proclaiming Marmaduke Emperor of Europe we crown an ideal, not a man; a principle, not flesh and blood.

"In Marmaduke we have an emperor from whom all human elements have been eliminated. He has no longer any personality which can be opposed, abused, or associated with ambition, mistakes, and perhaps crimes. He is the most powerful Emperor the world has ever seen, because he is invisible and invulnerable.

"Marmaduke's empire, like that of the Master

whom he has so well served, is infinitely mightier than any material empire.

"In proclaiming Marmaduke Emperor of Europe we recognise a new empire, a universal empire, a spiritual empire, the empire of righteousness and peace; and it is to such an emperor of such an empire that we now bow allegiance.

"It is only fitting that he who was primarily instrumental in the realisation of those grand ideals of universal righteousness, justice, peace, and progress, should be proclaimed Emperor of Europe, and practically conqueror of the world."

*   *   *   *   *   *

The Kaiser had finished speaking.

The ray of light still moved forward.

But Arthur's eyes were averted. Now he was gazing intently at the melancholy figure, the sole figure in mourning—Alicia.

After all, Arthur was only flesh and blood. He thought of happiness with Alicia. He thought of a home in which Alicia would form the centre and the circumference. He thought of that which he had never known—a possible fatherhood. He thought of a bold attempt to place Alicia on the throne of an already federated Europe.

He was on the point of springing forward; of declaring his identity; of putting an end to the horrible suspense, the unspeakable torture.

But what was that which caused Arthur to stop, which blanched his cheek and dammed the torrent of his thoughts in a moment?

The ray of light had changed. It no longer lost

itself in the dark space between the arches. It had encountered and lit up, with a thousand sparkling beams, a delicate piece of stone foliation. The ray of light scintillated in every direction until it blotted out everything else from Arthur's sight. Then, suddenly, in the centre of this glory of sunlight, he seemed to see the features of his lost Avis! Her face was spiritualised, etherealised; and as he looked he thought she smiled on him lovingly.

In a moment the whole scene, the pageant, Alicia, ambition, passion, earthly love, all were obliterated. The angel face in its aureole of sunlight, as it smiled, seemed again to beseech him to give up everything, even life itself, if thereby the cause might prosper.

He thought he could see the lips parting and hear the voice uttering those words he remembered so well:

"I am willing, as a separate entity, to become extinct, if the cause may benefit thereby."

Again—whether supernaturally or not—his dead wife supervened at a critical moment between him and temptation; protected him from himself, and saved him.

The ray of sunlight had shown him his lost love Avis, had illuminated his soul, had subdued his emotions, had thrown a flood of light on his past career, his present position, and his future path of duty. He now saw more clearly than he had ever seen before, how his self-obliteration was part of his life's great work. He saw how inevitable it was that the only opposing force which was able to combat and successfully overcome that force which had hitherto ruled the world—brute force—was a spiritual force.

As his earthly love, Alicia, faded from view, her place was taken by his heavenly love, Avis. For a moment he had caught a glimpse of that grand ideal connected with future existence—a reunion in soul with an angel wife. He was now tranquil and happy.

* * * * * *

The ceremony was nearly at an end. The Archbishop of Canterbury was repeating the Lord's Prayer. Arthur knelt with the others; the words fell upon his ear, but they were unheeded. He thought that he was again a little child and knelt at his mother's knee; she was stroking the fair hair of her beloved boy as he was repeating to her, in his childish tones, " Thy kingdom come ; Thy will be done on earth as in heaven."

Then there came a rushing noise in his head. He looked up. The place swam round. He knew no more. He had fainted.

* * * * * *

When Arthur returned to consciousness he found he was in the open air outside the Abbey. He looked up, and what first met his gaze were the black, curly locks, and the welcome face of his faithful friend, John Chapman, who was bending over him in tender solicitude.

* * * * * *

On the following day, *The Standard*, in commenting upon the interruption caused near the conclusion of the service by a man having fainted and having to be removed in an unconscious condition, said :

"It is neither more nor less than disgraceful that any man, or, for the matter of that, any woman, knowingly possessing either a weak heart, defective circulation, or a bilious temperament, should run the risk of creating a disturbance by attending any crowded function, especially of an exciting character."

EPILOGUE.

FIVE YEARS AFTER.—ON BOARD THE ORIENT LINER "CORANGAMITE." — THE REIGN OF MARMADUKE AND THE AGE OF GOLD.

FIVE years have elapsed since Arthur Hamilton was carried out of Westminster Abbey in an unconscious condition, and was taken under the ægis of his Fidus Achates, John Chapman.

We will, if you please, leave behind us those five years, with the vast social and political changes which have taken place during that period. We will also, if you please, give wings to our imagination, leave behind us Old England and her European neighbours, fly to southern antipodal climes, and alight on board the fine Orient liner *Corangamite*. She is bound for Sydney, New South Wales, and her lookout is hourly expecting to sight Port Jackson. Her passengers have given up those various temporary pursuits and occupations, serious or frivolous, by which time has been effectually killed during the tedium of a long sea voyage. Most are busily engaged either in making preparations to land, or in watching for the first glimpse of Port Jackson.

On the promenade deck, reclining in a comfortable

deck chair, is our old friend, Arthur Hamilton. He has made all his preparations for landing, and is reading, not for the first time, a recent number of *The Twentieth Century.*

He looks much older than when we last saw him; for he is palpably thinner, his hair is decidedly grey, his features are sharper and the lines on his face are considerably deeper. His expression is strongly suggestive of refined sadness, and his looks do not belie him. For he has been tempest-tossed on the billows of trouble; has weathered the storm and has finally reached port, but shorn of his strength and his glory; a wreck in all but the name. Although his eye has not entirely lost its fire, we look in vain for indications of the old familiar restless activity and indomitable energy.

We said Arthur was reading. It would have been more correct to say that he held the book in his hand and was gazing, with a far-away look, at the rising and falling waves.

Had he given audible expression to his thoughts, probably we should have heard him say: "I have finished my life's work on earth. I have fought and conquered. I rest and contemplate while I await the Master's summons. And then, again renewed vigour; again virile activity; again wonderful aspirations; the commencement of a glorious supernal life; then a soul union with my beloved Avis, never to be broken again."

Near him, still watching with wonder at the

ordinary routine work of the crew, as, indeed they had watched throughout the voyage, stand John Chapman and his wife.

The dream of this worthy couple is about to be fulfilled. They are going to Sydney to be near Althea and her husband.

Arthur has done it all. For, during five years' steady work upon *The East Anglian Daily Times*, he has saved enough money to accomplish his object. Moreover, through the kind offices of the grey-haired chief in Carr Street, he has obtained the refusal of a fairly good position on the staff of *The Sydney Morning Herald*, which still remains the oldest of the Australian daily newspapers.

And there was a home already awaiting the three emigrants. For the Editor of *The Herald*, had, with extreme thoughtfulness, provided a temporary home in the suburbs of Sydney; which home, if it suited Arthur and his two friends, could be taken as a permanent abode.

The two old people have grown young again. They know that there is no longer any need for them to work hard, or for the matter of that to work at all, for the household will consist of three persons only; their wants will be few, their habits simple; and Arthur insists upon taking over the entire financial charge of the household.

But neither Chapman nor his wife contemplates an idle life. The worthy woman will have plenty to do in the domestic administration of the tiny household. And there will always be numerous odds and ends of work about the house and garden to prevent the husband from being idle.

Certainly the old couple, in showing kindness to a person in distress, have entertained a veritable angel unawares. They are never tired of telling Arthur that he has repaid a thousand-fold what little they have done for him.

Chapman and his wife are never tired of inspecting, with awe-struck eyes, the wonderful structure which is their temporary habitation. Their experience of steamers had been limited to the Great Eastern boats which ply between Ipswich and Felixstowe Pier. But the magnificent appointments, the gigantic engines, the elaborate decorations, the great speed, of this fine steamer, are all so wonderful and mysterious, that the worthy pair not merely experience a new life ; they think they are in fairyland itself.

The *Corangamite* is the final triumph of the marine architect and engineer. The *Orient*, the *Austral*, the *Ormuz*, and the *Ophir*, have been as far surpassed as these, in their time, surpassed the old and obsolete liners.

It is not, therefore, surprising that Mr. and Mrs. Chapman wandered about, hand in hand like children, and experienced alternate emotions of awe and glee at the wonderful things they saw in connection with that mighty monster the *Corangamite*.

Did we say the two old people have grown young again ? Nay, they are fairly bubbling over with that enthusiastic, happy anticipation which it is said—quite erroneously—only belongs to children.

For when they are not absorbed in the wonders of the great ship, they are discussing and discussing and discussing again what they shall do when they again see their beloved daughter. They wonder how she will look; what she will say; what they will think of those two marvellous babies. Real live grandchildren who can talk and chatter as no babies ever talked and chattered before! What Althea and her husband and these same grandchildren will think of the numerous mysterious presents packed in no less mysterious boxes; the contents of which have never been divulged to a soul, not even to Mr. Arthur.

We said just now that Arthur held a book in his hand—a recent number of *The Twentieth Century*, The article he had been reading was upon "Marmaduke and his Work."

The eulogistic portion of this article does not cause Arthur to blush, for he has now become quite accustomed to regard Marmaduke as a separate entity and a higher personality than the humble Arthur Hamilton.

But what causes a flush to rise to his cheek, is the description by the author of the article—one of the most facile writers on the London Press, a nervous, sympathetic Irishman—of the enormous progress in Social Reform, the enormous development in the principles of international and commercial peace, and the consequent increase in the happiness of millions of people, which have resulted from what the writer aptly calls the " Reign of Marmaduke."

The writer shows how everything touched by the spirit of Marmaduke has changed as by the wand of a magician.

Marmaduke touched the Eastern Question, and a troublesome problem existed no more.

A well-ordered, well-administered Turkey, an autonomous kingdom under the protectorate of the united European Bund, grew up where an oppressive Oriental despotism of the most savage, barbaric type had previously existed. The Christians of Turkey were at last free from those nameless horrors of fiendish brutality which for so long a time had made the rule of the unspeakable Turk stink in the nostrils of the civilised world.

Marmaduke touched militarism, and it crumbled to dust, as Avis had foreseen.

Marmaduke touched commerce, and labour disputes became impossible and universal free trade was established.

Marmaduke touched the dark places of the earth, and they were at once illuminated with the glory of brotherhood, security, and contentment.

Marmaduke touched the consciences of the nations, and righteousness was recognised as the paying policy, selfishness the losing policy.

Marmaduke touched the hearts of the peoples, and there burst forth a glorious universal song of " Peace on earth and goodwill to men."

No wonder that the author of the article described the "Reign of Marmaduke" as the long-wished-for "Age of Gold."

The article concluded thus:

"The startling policy of the Emperor of Germany in regard to Alsace-Lorraine was the commencement of a new epoch in the history of the world. Imperialism and Radicalism joined hands, and that union was cemented by righteousness and truth.

"Such a union meant the universal reign of the common people, tempered by the safeguards afforded by constitutional monarchy.

"Let not the Anglo-Saxon feel jealous that to the Teuton has fallen the task of leading the van in the world's progress. It is true that the hand of the Teuton was the first to strike the fetters from nations enslaved by militarism; but the brain which directed and controlled that hand was the brain of the Anglo-Saxon.

"It is true that the Emperor of Germany, the great champion of right, is the chosen chief of his European co-rulers; but it must not be forgotten that Marmaduke is still Emperor of Europe. It is an Anglo-Saxon who rules the world."

THE END.

www.ingramcontent.com/pod-product-compliance
Lightning Source LLC
Chambersburg PA
CBHW031933230426
43672CB00010B/1908